When Cinderbella Gets Divorced

The True Story of a Woman Who Goes in Search to Find 'The Purposes of Life' while she Touches the Pains that Came from Saying the Vows of "I Do".

Deanne Kim

Nebulae Productions and Booksellers CC.
P.O. Box 440,
Ngodwane,
1209,
Mpumalanga Province,
South Africa

Email Address: nebulae@xwi.co.za

ISBN: 978-1-77572-188-8

Layout & Design: Candice Pierce
Cover Design: Robert Mackintosh

--------- *Acknowledgements* ------

For my daughter Candice, sister Maryanne and all those precious souls that have acted out their roles on this stage of my life's journey. - I wish to humbly acknowledge how grateful I am that each one of you was casted to assist in my personal growth.

I give thanks to the Higher Powers and Light-beings for their protection and wisdom that they bestowed on us all.

And so it has been told that '*in the end it doesn't really matter*' and I truly pray that we will all return to this same *source* when we lay our decaying bodies back into the womb of our mother earth and fly our souls to our real home and live happily forever after.

Contents

---*Prologue*---

This book was never written with the intention that '*someday baby, you will be classified or labelled as a famous writer*'. The gifts that were bestowed upon my life as a *being* were guided from a '*higher light*' and hence I am grateful and humbled to share my own life's lessons without an '*ego*'.

My greatest rewards would be to *feel* that whoever chooses to comprehend and view these '*acts*' would experience a shift in their own personal life and thereby 'walk a path that is rewarding and fulfilling' – to me it's known as 'Life'- and factually the opposite of life is death. The 'gift' that I was given of having my life extended, (which I will explain in this book) has been the greatest 'gift' and therefore all additional factors have become unimportant due to being exposed to their worthlessness while facing death's call!

It has been a wonderful experience as an author of over 60 South African Educational books to have the privilege of '*feeling*' what was personally needed to express, without having to conform to the mundane structure that I generally follow while writing under a 'certified curriculum'. My wishes are that whoever glances over these memories, or touches the surfaces of my expression may be greatly blessed, while they follow their *own* calling and dance toward the unity that we all one day will share.

This book is divided into two performances. The first being my personal interpretation of the *game of life* and the second an additional optional choice for the reader to encounter their own '*mirroring the self*' exercises as they act out *life's play*.

i

----𝒟𝒾𝑜𝑔𝓇𝒶𝓅𝒽𝓎----

Deanne Kim, born and raised in South Africa, studied art for a total of 12 years. Art has taken her on a phenomenal journey, wherein she has taught formal art classes internationally whilst residing in the Philippines; as well as in her home country for a total of 20 plus years. Whilst studying through UNISA (University of South Africa), she branched into a new way of teaching, thus developed her 'Art Therapy' classes, which originated in Johannesburg in 1998. As an Artist, Publisher and 'Therapist', Deanne's love for children and passion for life has led her to write and illustrate educational books ranging from Grade R – 12, collectively resulting in over 60 Educational books produced to date. Deanne's zest for life, writing, teaching and passion never ceased after she was diagnosed with terminal cancer in 1993. Given a second chance has been the greatest gift and she wants to share what she has discovered with all whom cross her path. Through her own life's journey, she began writing and expressing her experiences –from this, she compiled two separate yet integrated books – *'When Cinderbella Gets Divorced'* and *'The Cracked Slipper'*.

Performance1.

------- The Game of Life -------

1

HEINOUS?

Praise be to thee,
Nonconformist,
Woman
sacrificial saboteur
who ran the gauntlet
relinquished social security
recruited justice
cut the veil
on all cylinders
you burnt the books
smashed the glass slipper
and victoriously screamed
I AM!

Hail be to thee
Goddess of freedom
Unchained spirit
who rides hell for leather.
Life giver of heads or tails
Exempt from sarcastic flies
and hypocritical corpses.
They smother your dream no more
You are who you are
purposely convinced,
Immortal temptress.

In Every Female

In every female there is a magical seed that longs to be watered by
an elemental lover
Comforted and sheltered by the universal skies
Fed and clothed by Mother Nature's splendour
'til the day that she unfolds her petals
and opens up to embrace the sun

There comes a time in a woman's life that she throws her glass slipper against the oval mirror and screams to herself "I'm going beyond!" She makes the decision to follow her heart, to discard the cracks, to stop patching her make-up and goes in search of more. She begins her quest for TRUTH.

Standing in the emotionless hallway Cinderbella made her choice - it was final - *it was over*! The circle had been broken – her heart was torn. She had sacrificed her *all* for something that was no longer *real*. She had to cut the ties and free herself from these prison chains and wedding bands and go in search of *freedom*. Where was that land of make-believe – did it ever really exist - was this all a dream or the world of reality?
Holding her head high she looked to the skies and screamed – *I AM*!

Cinderbella grew up in a small *coastal hamlet*, close to the sound of the ocean's murmurs, played with Hermit crabs and walked barefoot on the silver sand. Her parents, you could say, were from the upper class bracket. They had resided in many beautiful homes. Life was never tough and they had a domestic for every occasion.

Cinderbella's mother, a thoroughbred and extrovert, was popular amongst the community folk and certainly knew how to entertain. Cinderbella on the other hand was withdrawn and shy. Her wealth lay inside her head. Cinderbella was a true princess, or should I say *in her world she was*. Even though she was an introvert, she loved performing in plays. During her Primary School days' younger students would sit on the embankment and experience a *world of fantasy* as a few of the children acted out fantastical realities.

These were the times that she was allotted to act out her *reality* by taking on an alternative character. It was no longer her – it was an innovative figurine that conversed in an abrupt manner yet graciously acted the pompous part.

This Cinderbella had no ugly sisters. Her brother was considered to be the faultless son and her seventeen-year younger baby sister occupied her parent's life.

Cinderbella's inquisitive mind enticed her to seek answers that were not readily available to the *masses*. What were the truths that she so ached for – were they hidden in the pictorials from the bedtime stories books that her mother habitually read to her every night before she dropped off into her own fairyland?

One night at the age of four Cinderbella was magically awoken by an image that resembled no humanlike form and radiated the entire room. Cinderbella was astounded. This must be the fairy godmother! There was no wand, carriage, coachman or prince – just a presence that was indescribably beautiful and serene. As she gazed at this light formation it spoke to her in a gentle reassuring voice. It told her that it was coming back to fetch her one day. How amazing – her very own Caretaker! She was too young to understand the meaning, but held on to this experience throughout her life. An occurrence as small as this can be an anchor when you need it, she found this out on numerous occasions throughout her guided life.

At the age of 26 she married a Professional Golfer; her parents were delighted that their daughter had eventually *"seen the light"* after previously dating so many weird and wonderful characters.
He had fallen in love with her because of her uniqueness. Cinderbella was his new found treasure and he promised to cherish her forever.

Cinderbella recalls the time when she was twenty-four and invited to watch him play a professional tournament. The prize money was high and the professionals were all mentally focused to win. She had never walked around a golf course before. Everything seemed so flawless to the extent that even the grass appeared to be cut precisely to the exact millimetre. As she walked she conjectured whether or not these sportsmen where even in the least bit attentive of the natural beauty that surrounded them outside these precincts. It was intriguing to see how they lived in their diminutive worlds of *golf.* How could this white ball create so much anxiety on their very existence? Did they ever practice living in the moment without distressing about the final outcome? By the fifteenth hole Cinderbella was bored stiff. She sat on the embankment and watched the show. Running her fingers through the grass she came across a bee. It was tired and thirsty. "I have been put onto its path to help it!" she thought to herself. She leaped up to find a flower; broke the stamen open and the bee began to suck. In her mind she knew it needed liquid and that she had to be its life's rescuer. Charles and her hadn't spoken for fifteen holes, instead Cinderbella had walked silently near him and watched, but now was the time that she needed him to understand the bee's crucial state. Walking up to him on the putting green she whispered in his ear "Do you think that there's any ways you guys can hurry up 'cause I've got a bee that's busy dying and I need to get a drink for it at the club house urgently?". He stood there speechless, not sure if she was joking or if this was an insane female that he had invited along to watch a Million Dollar golf tournament!

None the less two years later they were married.

In Cinderbella's mind she had rehearsed the part of being this beautiful bride a billion times over and imagined how her groom would be waiting for her as she walked down the aisle. She had smelt the fabric of her wedding gown and tasted the flowers that she would carry. This would be the day that she made her never-ending vows, ascend into the coach with her prince and waved her wedding ring from the carriage window for all to see! She would journey to the castle and together they would enter a fantastical world where they would make passionate love and live happily ever after - Happily forever?

Little did she know what the future held and after only four months of married life things changed drastically.

ACT TWO

----*The Right to Choose*----

Shortly after their wedding Charles had gone from strength to strength. He had won three major tournaments consecutively. They decided to save up and move to America for a short time where he would then be able to participate in the American Golf Circuit.

Everything was glamorous and blissful; nothing could ever fracture their world. Children were out of the question as Charles firmly believed that his success depended on staying mentally focused without having any additional distractions or irritations. Her world on the other hand consisted of playing the perfect *golfer's wife* and therefore she put every crumb of energy into ensuring that the hotel bookings were made, suitcases were packed and unpacked rigorously and monotonously. They spent about three days out of each month in their own townhouse and the remainder experiencing different hotels.

People often asked Cinderbella what it was like being a golfer's wife and whether living out of suitcases bothered her. She knew no alternative and therefore assumed that this was part of the *deal* of being married to a sportsman. It was fun - she encountered many different places, met interesting people and never had to cook dinner.

At the age of 26 she obviously hadn't got to know much about the average married woman's life other than being a golfer's wife. Out of all the norms that the average wife would have to date experienced, Cinderbella's most dramatic encounter was when Charles first dumped a huge pile of golfing trousers on the scullery table and asked her to wash and iron them. She stared at him and felt her last blood vessel melt uncompromisingly into outer space. Was this part of the deal? Yes, she supposed it must be, so she picked up the phone and called her mother who now lived seven hours away from her.

The city life felt greyer now than ever before and as she stared out of the townhouse window she noticed the unbending buildings clenching their fists as the wind tried to outwit them.

There were no more hermit crabs or ocean sounds to relieve her thoughts. All that mattered now was to get these stupid militant nylon trousers ironed before the prince returned.

"Darling," said Cinderbella's mother on the other end of the receiver "let's start from the very beginning. Can you see a plug at the end of the iron? Now you need to put it into the wall plug and turn the switch on." Cinderbella realised that her mother had probably never ironed in her life before and was now trying to teach her daughter something that she needed to someday teach herself.

With every stroke of the iron a new tear was born. How she longed to be back home in her comfortable little enchanted village, and be mollycoddled – if not by her parents then undoubtedly by her nature friends that she so longed for.

Cooking she soon found out, was another of her weak points. Having been a vegetarian since the age of fifteen she had become content eating raw foods. Why on earth would a health conscious sportsman need any more than this? Well she was wrong. This mentally strong-minded man needed meat - and meat she had to cook. Yet again another disastrous outcry as she resentfully cooked his first "meaty meal". Why the hell hadn't her mother ever taught her that you did not have to poach sausages until they were skinless and swam aimlessly around in a huge frothing consommé? Why would anyone want to take an animals life anyway? In *her* world animals had souls, spoke to her about their feelings and became a brother or sister on a regular basis – they were her other family!

Day dreamingly Cinderbella flashed back into the time when she was much younger. Silently she observed herself sitting on the rocks watching the tiny innocent fish swim aimlessly around in a rock pool before its death. She had caused this death after dangling it from her red fishing rod that proudly hooked this life-force away from it origination. Now the rock pool had become its new home – an environment friendly prison cell - but still it swam frantically in anticipation that someday, somehow it would reach the light at the end of the tunnel and return to paradise.
She felt it crying and yelling for all its friends and family that it had been kidnapped from. Why had she been so cruel? Was she going to eat this life or place it back into its world of truth? It died before she could make the crucial decision but from that day on Cinderbella knew *she had the right to choose*.

The overflowing broth from the frying pan hurled her back to reality.

ACT THREE

--------*The Game of Life*--------

This tournament was going to mean a lot to Charles. It was known as a *'knockout match play'* - which by now Cinderbella had learnt all about. He had made it into the semi-finals and was on a winning streak. They had tried all types of methods that would assist Charles to stay calm and collective. Every book that Cinderbella read was based on techniques to help her beloved husband win. *Eat to win – you are what you eat – the secret of success – success is the secret – live to die –die to live –* who the hell cares as long as it made a difference. When a golfer has a good day then the rest of the world smiles with him!

It was 7 am and the day had come for Charles's big challenge. He woke up and made coffee, he always did and it had somewhat become a *control thing*.

Cinderbella lay in bed staring out of the hotel room's window thinking about how beautiful it was to observe what others so often took for granted - The sunlight that sprinkled fairy dust onto the earths clothing and the melodies that harmoniously echoed from the creature beings as they gave thanks to the breaking dawn.

Suddenly there was a piercing thud in the kitchen.

"Is everything okay?" she asked as she sneered and thought that maybe Charles had accidentally put his finger in the plug and now paying off some *karmic* lesson for making her iron those silly pants.

There was a sense of coldness in the silence.

Maybe she should take back her wicked thoughts – or maybe not!

Cinderbella gracefully removed her satin sheets, peeked at herself in the golden bedroom mirror, smiled and floated flirtatiously toward the area where she assumed her prince charming would most probably be blowing off the ashes from his neatly manicured nails and waiting for princess charming to come kiss him all better.

Much to her horror it was not so. Instead he lay dead-looking and paralysed on the floor.

Frantically she picked up the phone and instructed the medics to come to her rescue.

No time for mascara darling this is for real! Bugger the high heels, nipple caps, lingerie or *Dior* handbag; she had to get Charles to see the light! The seconds felt like hours as they raced to the nearest hospital some ninety kilometres away.

No longer was he in his little comfort zone of *eat to win or up your kilt thing-a-ma-jig,* a new game of life was challenging him directly in his face.

Was this the successful day that he had waited for?

Charles underwent a seven hour operation after a malignant tumour was diagnosed. The doctors explained to Cinderbella that she would have to accept that her husband would be paralysed for the rest of his life.

His left side was completely lame and as she nursed him in that hospital bed she vowed to herself that she would not accept this present negative situation and believed that he would be healed. He had to, she wanted him to and therefore her faith was all she had left to hold onto. This play was for real. Cinderbella knew that without having a prince that was able to get back on his feet and be healthy again, their life would have to change drastically. There would be no more American Golf Tournament dreams if she could not manipulate this scene.

Day and night she bathed and fed him as he lay lamely in their bed half paralysed.

After many hours of sleeplessness, Cinderbella knew that the only way she could change the plot was to change the scene.

Driving to her home town with a paralysed prince she realised that she had to touch base again – the sea sand that revitalises all limpness – her and Charles would need to walk barefoot in the sand.
Do you still believe in miracles – well she does - after only one month of positive projection, prayer and intervention, Charles began hitting golf balls again. Doctors were amazed and yes, somewhere in her fantastical mind, Cinderbella was too.

Thirteen months after being married Cinderbella's daughter was born.
Besides her wedding this was one event that she had really wished for. She felt as though they were a real family and being a mother became a gratifying experience.
Cinderbella's days were occupied by this new life and Charles had decided to branch into golf course designing.
With these new decisions came new lessons – hard lessons. They spent less and less time together and Cinderbella sensed that the closeness that they once had was slowly being replaced by more seemingly important obligations. At first she told herself that it must be part of the whole marriage deal. Strange how before they got married they used to sit in a restaurant and scan through various couples at nearby tables as they played the guessing game. This meant deciding which of the couples were married and which were not. Cinderbella and Charles used to laugh at their own conclusions - miserable people who rarely talk were the definite married couples. They had vowed to themselves that the day they got married they

would make it one of their top priorities to keep a special spark to their relationship and never allow this cold non-verbal communication to enter their ordeal. They believed that they would show the world how Cinderbella and her prince lived happily ever after – could live –should live – and prove it.

Maybe it was the new addition - or maybe due to the fact of her body being a little fuller after having a baby – maybe this had changed his desires - who knows. All she knew was that it was different now and she began to yearn for love.

Many nights went by and Cinderbella lay frigidly next to her prince charming questioning her own mind about where things had gone wrong. Was it because Charles had come from a home that was minimal affectionate? Cinderbella's mother-in-law was like a 'functional object' and robotically performed her daily wife duties in a strict, methodical manner. Cinderbella's family on the other hand were warm and loving. Her mother had always taught her never to go to bed carrying anger and that if there were any discrepancies it was vital that they be sorted out before retiring. Maybe it was just a fable but yet this seemed to have worked for her parents so why wasn't it working for her in this marriage. She was perceived as totally insane if she dared question why their love had changed.

Lucinda their daughter had become Cinderbella's pillar of strength. Much to her mother-in-law's horror, Lucinda was almost three years old and still breastfeed! Was it a comfort for Lucinda or Cinderbella – who really knows? Marriage life was still a subliminal worry and by this stage communication was virtually null and void. The moral of this dilemma was for certain - they were drifting apart.

Cut – cut – please cut – this isn't how it is supposed to be! Wasn't Cinderbella assigned the role to be a happy princess? Someone or some hex is definitely playing a mind game with this tale.

Well sorry, chum, the story continues.

As in most cases and similar life incident that transpires in human relationships, they discuss having another child. Cinderbella merrily assumed that this would at last fulfil the emptiness that she previously experienced. So off to the *gynie* she goes to ensure that all her body parts are still intact. No big bad wolf was going to huff and puff this hag down!

Drama, drama, one of those shocking calls screams for her attention - you know the one that tells some unlucky woman that they have an abnormality appearing in their pap smear? Every woman dreads this call and now it was her turn. It was a few weeks before her 30th birthday and no she wasn't an old hag – she was gorgeous!

Being diagnosed with Fourth stage Cervix Cancer; doctors recommend that she undergo a hysterectomy as soon as possible. Wow what a shock, maybe they had mistaken her cells with someone else's. She needed time to think – think and pray – or maybe just run away from this realisation. Having her womb removed would mean no more children, and this was clearly the opposite reason for her previous visit to the gynaecologist.

She had lost a lot of weight by this stage, but had originally put it down to the fact that she was unhappy. Once again Cinderbella yearned to walk barefoot in the sand. She needed to hear the sound of the ocean and feel the wind blow through her hair. She just needed to 'feel' - feel what she longed for.

As she stood on the banks of her hometown beach, she did not have the energy to transport her painful frail body to the silver sands that

14

she so yearn to walk barefoot onto. She was aware that she was fading away. This was no joke – she was scared – not scared of death but scared of the unknown.

What would happen to Lucinda – she was too young to be without a mother - she needed to live even if it was for this very reason.

Once again Cinderbella was put to the test - this time she was at stake! She had to become focused –believe, have faith and accept that she will be healed. Now let me just stop the story here and ask you if you truly know what it feels like to be in a crisis dilemma where you are faced with a life-threatening scenario and have to make a crucial decision and go against all odds? Well if so you will understand that it's as much as placing your bets on black or white on a gambling game and hoping that you make the right gut feel choice!

After much introspection, Cinderbella made the choice to tell the doctors they can wait! She believed that another miracle would happen – after all that was her 'real' world. She would take on the challenge to walk the road of *faith* once again.

Her grandmother had always been a mother figure in Cinderbella's life. She was an amazing woman and although she never attended church services, her belief system was strong. One evening *granny* had the desire to attend a meeting at the local church; it was during the time of her granddaughter's new diagnosed illness. While sitting in a reserved manner, the minister stops the gathering and asked the congregation "Is there is anyone here who has a loved one that has cancer? If so, I want you to please come forward now".
Cinderbella's grandmother knew that she was being looked after and plucked up the courage to stand-in for her beloved grand-daughter.

An old used handkerchief was prayed over and couriered to Cinderbella. This ritual had to become a step in faith. Cinderbella could either decide to say "hey silly old pastor, maybe you should have first washed your hanky before making me trust in your believe?" – alternatively you could take it as a loving and precious gift, believing that the energy that it held was going to make her all better. The choice was hers and in order to make an event effective she had to apply an action.

Every morning Cinderbella would open the curtains, place the handkerchief on her lower abdomen and believe that she was going to get better. She had so much to live for, if not for her broken down marriage, then at least for the beautiful daughter she had received as a gift from the Great Creator.

Vowing that she would never ever allow another man to make her unhappy again, she promised herself that she would annul this situation of their unhappy marriage from her mind. There was no way that she would allow hurt to *eat her up*.

Three months later – as previously declared - she scheduled a reassessment appointment with her gynaecologist and yes, yes, yes – miracles did exist - all signs of cervix cancer had disappeared and she was completely healed!

ACT FOUR

------ Incarnated ------

EMBODIED

HAND

Tightly squeezed - no blood will flow.
Nails slice flesh - blood to glow
Cold – no life
Blood – the warmth.

TEETH

Locked together – no speech
Crushed – the sound
Pain – the silence
Unity – the freedom

EYES

Stare without vision
Blackness – escape
Dryness – emotion
Blindness – eternity

HEART

Anxious pulsation
Throbs the blade
Beats the pain
I never really made.

17

By 1994 Cinderbella had fully recovered. Her marriage was still the same, but I suppose in a way she had 'moved on' and no longer allowed the worry of her empty marriage to hinder her. Instead she occupied herself with interests that stimulated her positively and fed her mind, body and soul with things that *really* mattered.

One of Cinderbella's sacrificed passions was painting. She loved art and before marrying she worked in many Graphic Studios. Cinderbella painted on a regular basis as this gave her a sense of uniqueness. To her, Artists were unusual and interesting people. They lived their life according to the seasons. They were temperamental and yet created a world that many I'm sure would have loved to live in. This had been her world - a world of fantasy - playing and living each moment for what it was. Nothing else had mattered. Nothing existed besides this craziness of experiencing a creative day.

Looking back she realised how she had sold her soul in order to become a mother, wife and responsible woman. She dressed differently, spoke differently, lived differently and yes in the process had almost killed herself by trying to perfect these unfamiliar roles. What she was yearning for was to find *herself* again. She needed to reclaim what she had lost, yet wondered if it would be possible to be a mother, wife and still miraculously have a life of her own.

The strangest incident happened shortly after her Cancer diagnosis. While pushing her daughter in the grocery trolley she bumped into an old boyfriend. They used to work together before she got married. It was amazing to see him again and as they sat drinking coffee he asked "Are you happy? You seemed to have changed. Do you still paint?" Cinderbella sat there dumbfounded with a million thoughts going through her head. There was no way to explain all her life's experiences since the last time they had seen each other.

18

Life had definitely changed, she had changed, she was not happy and no she did not paint anymore! That was it - she knew she had to find that *lost* person again. Was it in actual fact 'herself' she was longing for - not another baby or a husband to love her or this or that - just her *true* self!

Cinderbella enrolled into an art class and every Tuesday and Thursday morning she would sit with other like-minded people and yes, paint.

Oddly enough Charles began to notice the difference. He could see the spark that twinkled in her eyes and smell the oils on her skin from a distance. Even so it made no difference to their marriage and the relationship seemed to be likened to a worm that gnawed away at an apple. Many nights Cinderbella lay wondering if he would ever be able to hold her like he used to, or if one day she would awaken and find that she had been having a nightmare and that everything was as it should have been - would have loved to be - and they lived happily ever after, forever.

Men to her had become strange creatures; she just couldn't figure them out. What did they *really* want? She had played the 'perfect golfer's wife', performed the 'pregnant princess' stunt, groomed the floors and poached the slaughtered lambs. What more were women supposed to present on a titanium platter to their princes?

Charles had climbed the corporate ladder up in his field of Golf Course Designing and soon offered an opportunity to administer an overseas Gary Player Project. Hooray, they were moving to the Philippines! Maybe this would be a blessing in disguise and they would soon announce themselves as the 'comprehensive family' in a new country stage performance - what an amazing prize!

19

In her mind she visualized that this was the event that the worm left their apple and that they as a couple become whole and juicy once more!

Cinderbella's parents were so excited for them. Her mom kept emphasising that she only packs only *Island-life clothing*. Sarongs should be a 'must' on her *to-take-list*.
The prince, princess and three year old toddler sell their home and furniture, hug their animals' goodbye and embark on a December flight to *fairyland*.

Even though Cinderbella knew she had to put on her 'strong face' and smile - it still felt traumatic and a sense of loss somehow frightened her. Leaving behind all your comfort and not knowing what lies ahead or where you are going can make you feel quite off balance if you haven't done it before.
Even though her parents had loved renovating houses and therefore had moved quite a few times, she had never relocated to another country. Well now she had a first-hand experience.
During her many lonely hours Cinderbella had prayed to the fairies, gods or whoever she thought was out there, to show her what her true life's purpose was, and maybe this was the first steps to her finding out – well we'll have to wait and see.

Arriving in Manila, the capital of Luzon - an island in Philippines – was quite a culture shock. It was smoggy, hot and overpopulated. Cinderbella wondered if her mother had the faintest idea what she was talking about. This wasn't another Hawaiian Island where people walked around with sarongs and pretty flower dangling from their sunbathed necks. It was polluted - over populated – surreal! Everyone looked cloned - about five foot tall, with brown eyes and black hair. They scared her with their overfriendliness; she being a

South African came from a culture that had a more reserved mannerism and generally 'Johannesburg city humans' didn't care a damn about other similar *two-legged* names or telephone numbers. These must be the people that her mother had warned her about in her early childhood when she firmly instructed her "*never to speak to strangers*". Now at the age of thirty, Cinderbella was being invaded by these '*child-abusers*'!

For Lucinda's sake, who had just turned four in September, Cinderbella had to act as if she was unruffled and reassurance her that everything was normal - normal, just like the way her father and mother pompously smiled at each other.

ACT FIVE

------ *The Porcupine Quill.* ------

Deciding whether or not to write this book took me over three years. I needed an answer, not just a yes/no answer, but one that was spiritually acknowledged by a *higher force*. Over the past three years I have spoken to many women and shared their common hurts while they underwent hardships and turmoil's in their marriage. Undoubting we all had one thing in common... *anger*. Anger towards the fact that we had sacrifice so much of our years - whether it was because of our husbands needing our support, giving up our careers, looking after children, playing the *good wife* part or merely choosing to keep a balance in the home by becoming the home-maker. I originally decided that the *When Cinderbella gets Divorced* book would express all these angers and encourage woman to take a stand, and say *"I also have rights"* and learn to live a long earned 'whole" life once again. Things have changed....

I wake up early Saturday morning, by now after questioning my mind a billion times whether or whether not to start writing this book, I sit quietly in my small meditation room. David, my new husband that I have been married to for the past ten years, has been pleading with me to change my life and start doing something I would love to do rather than what I declare to *have to do*. Having an analytical nature like I do, I first need clarity - real clarity. Focusing on my breathing and space that I occupy, I clear my mind and bring my attention to the stillness *within* me. In this moment in time I need an answer. Stating my intentions and requisitions to the Great Spirit I ask to be guided and shown the true answer. I announce "I will write the book on condition that I find a porcupine quill". How I came to the bizarre assumption of using a porcupine quill as a sign I didn't even question. It just happened. Focusing my intent and desires I give thanks to the universe for acknowledging my request.

Some humans have no patience; I admit I fall into that category! Seconds later, in the early hours of that morning, I was already searching the garden for a porcupine quill. Of course I did not find one and nor the following morning. By midday I had told David that I had a surprise for him, all he had to do was be ready to do something exciting by five o' clock that evening. I had packed a picnic basket; here I should mention that when I say packed the picnic basket it included everything from a table cloth to the smallest imaginable item that in most cases would never have been thought of including. As we walked along the path to the edge of the escarpment, which is about a half an hours walk form our home, David complained about the excessive weight of what he had to carry. In my mind this was supposed to have been one of those long overdue romantic strolls where lovers stared at each other as they held hands and whispered sweet I love you.

It was beautiful once we had finally reached the top after much sweat and pain and we sat quietly waiting for the sun to slide gently behind the mountain. Over ten years ago we had walked up the same path to say our marriage vows. Time goes past so quickly, and before you know it another day has come to an end. Darkness starts creeping into the evening and we slowly start our decline. The mountain offers much magical and sometimes strange energy. Over the past few years I had spent many hours walking and observing its surroundings thereby becoming quite familiar with each individual

23

path that led to different outcomes. Walking down with a less laden picnic basket we come to a Y-junction and have to make the decision which one of the two paths to follow. David says right and I say left, obviously we take the right! Only two days ago had it been new moon and therefore the night skies are dark. We get lost, very lost! By this time I have written the romance off to a bad-made decision. We are both irritated by now, David by my sarcastic remarks of "I told you so" and me by his misjudgement. My torch is going flat as I skim through the tall grass to find a familiar path. Why was it that every time I expected something to turn out just the way I wanted it to, did it have to land up being a total disaster!

And there unexpectedly do I find it! The porcupine quill, laying amongst the long tall grass on this dark black night! I was speechless, because I had not mentioned the Saturday morning meditation episode to David, and also, this was one moment in time that I would least expect to find my answer!

Tears ran down my cheeks as I realised how often I had tried to play god. Many times I thought I was the one that knew all the answers to how, what and when a situation or question should be taken care of. In this case I was taught that *in order to find I had to first get 'lost'*.

ONE WHO LOVES

One who loves truly
is always filled with the nectar
from his lovers flower,
the sap embraces his being with eternal warmth.
She nurtures his soul with sunshine
And feeds him with everlasting smiles of reassurance,
That he and she are truly part of the wholeness of
Immortal love...
Forever

ACT SIX

--------*Having a Child*-------

Having a child from my previous marriage has taught me many lessons. After almost twelve years after being divorced, Charles, myself and our daughter sit together for lunch. This is not an unfamiliar event as we have sat together to discuss numerous topics in the past. But somehow this day turns out to be totally different to what I had expected. Learning to *go with the flow* of what life's lessons often takes a lot of practice and my lesson began to by learning how should *stop expecting.*

It has only been a few days from when I had found my porcupine quill and yes shortly after commencing to write this book. It's Charles's 49th birthday and the three of us sit around one of the local restaurant's table. We seem to be like the three little dickey birds, sitting on the tree wondering which one of us will be the first to fly away. By now Lucinda has grown to be a beautiful young lady. As we sit talking about the normal mundane things in our lives, I mention to him that I've started writing my book. He's fascinated and questions its contents. "You're in it", I say smiling.

For over an hour we interact and reminisced all the events that we have gone through. It turns out to be the weirdest experience. I had hated him after the divorce - had so much anger towards his cruelty that he had 'thrown in my face' - resented the way he treated Lucinda as though she was a small child where in actual fact she was old enough to make her own decisions in life without his permission.

And there we sat, discussing the past as though we had been watching a movie together.

It was fascinating to watch this man have tears in his eyes as he said 'how amazing our life has been and isn't it fantastic that we've all *grown* so from our mistakes.'

Life is a journey and yet when we are riding the terrifying waves of a particular momentary storm, we can rarely begin to imagine that it will all settle down and return to becoming a peaceful gentle ocean.

RECONNECTING TIME

Time is like a thief
That vanishes into the blackness of the night,
Skilfully stealing precious jewels of life's breath.

We walked alongside,
You're much older now,
And yes, so am I,
Your arm around my aged body,
Time has passed us by.

Your eyes shine like virgin diamonds
Uncut by life's scars
Your blood is of mine
But your soul is ever free.

Where did time go?

27

You so silently became woman
Only yesterday I bathed and held you
To my breast.
We laugh
As we share
The memories of history
But silently
I suppress a tear
A tear that yearns
To hold onto this memory.

"Mother, my mother",
you whisper my name lovingly,
"Let time be time,
A season of death and birth,
Soon I will be same as you,
But for now let's stop
the stars and moon
Dance with me as we
Reconnect time."

ACT SEVEN

Journeying

Journeying back to South Africa after spending over a year and a half in the Philippines held many new changes, changes that neither Charles nor I had ever expected. We had locked our homes doors and expected to return in a few weeks once the golf course project commenced - little did we discern that it would be the last time we ever saw it again.

Living in a foreign country offers many new challenges. I had joined the arts guild and made friends with the locals. They were fascinating, humble people. Their way of life was different to ours and their expectations and needs minimal. With the frequent earthquakes and typhoons, one tended to become content with simpler living. I grew to understand that life was precious and that at any time Mother Nature could destroy what I considered to be precious. A certain amount of detachment had taken place in my life and I began to appreciate each new day as though it was my first. Having gone through cancer - both the malignant brain tumour of Charles's and the cervix cancer of mine - I tried figure out the puzzles of our lives.

Our relationship had strengthened while being away from our familiarities. Somehow there seemed to have been a shift. We were not as close as we were before his brain tumour, but I began to accept that maybe this is how marriage was and that being in love most probably was always just a momentary infatuation.

Meeting traditional healers had become an interesting aspect of living in this Asian country. Pete and his wife practiced an aura cleansing technique and having an enquiring mind I had decided to attend their humble space twice a week. On arrival they would place a bowl of salt water close to my seat. Pete would begin with a simple prayer and then work hypnotically with the apparently called '*energy fields*' that he believed surrounded my body. This was all new to me and I never closed my eyes for one split second just in case they did some *hockey pokey* trick to try and deceive me or convert me into some *Eastern philosophy or religious mass cult*! It was fascinating for me to analytically observe how the clear bowl of water that was placed on my arrival actually changed colour and transformed into a muddy brown pigmentation. Rather than question this phenomena I preferred to enjoy the peacefulness that replaced my previous anxiousness. My journey had started at the early age of four but my yearning for life's *real purpose* was increasing daily.

As we boarded our flight back to South Africa little did I anticipate that my *life's purpose* was going to unfold new *tests yet gifts*.

And so my new *act* began.

It was strange to me how relationships could change like the seasons. One minute I could *feel* happy like a blossom that danced with the refreshing breeze of spring and the next as though every leaf had fallen off my tree.

On our return we visited Charles's parents and then moved in to my parent's home. All prior arrangements had been put on hold and we were notified that it would probably take a few months before they needed us to return to our home in the Philippines. In the interim they offered Charles a substitute position in a mining community for nine months. I was devastated that we could not first return to collect our belongings before beginning this temporary venture. Mining community – it sounded horrific! What was I supposed to learn from this lesson, how to pan for gold?

BIZARRE

Collecting,
Hoarding,
Saving,
Preservation perspires pompously our pride and pains.

Stressing,
Exhausting,
Worrying,
Affirming anxiously ambiguity of our autonomous aims.

Working,
Laboriously,
Mechanically.
Pretentiously proud paupers we pamper our paths.

Vandalising,
Destroying,
Wasting,
Mechanically mesmerised merchandise we mime man.

Stealing,
Raping,
Lying,
Rectifying religiously ruptured rivalry of rights.

Mankind,
Vultures,
Thieves,
Slither sinfully silently into your insanity.

ACT SIX

------ *First Boyfriend* ------

My first boyfriend was David. I adored him and even though I was eight when I first met him, something inside me felt like I could be his little friend for life. I recall the first time he kissed me, I was twelve and even so I knew that this was love at first sight. His father was the local doctor in the town where we lived and yet my parents were always sceptical of this boy. When my parents to a new country which in those days it was called Rhodesia, I feared that we would never see each other again.

Four years later we accidentally our paths cross. There seemed to be no time span. Our love felt as strong as it was when we were separated by distance. David had just finished his military service and I had two more years before graduating from High school. To me at this vulnerable age he was absolutely the most handsome *Ken* I could have imagined,

With regard to my parents nothing had changed and they still would not approve of him. He was told he could sleep in his car in our driveway, but under no circumstances anywhere under our roof. I knew that this type of relationship could go nowhere and after spending two days together reconnecting he left to go back to Pretoria where he would further his studies. That was the last time I had any contact with him even though I so often wondered what had become of his life.

Strange how life turns out - my parents had moved back to the same town as where David's parents had lived for many years. By this time I was thirty three, married, with a child, and going to spend time with my parents before Charles's new *mining project*. One day bumping into David's mother in town she invites me for tea. I was nervous but yet my curiosity lures me to have enough courage to pay her a visit. David I am told has been living with a woman for the past ten years, married once or twice before and not in a very good *head space*. He will be coming down to visit his mother in a few days' time and consequently I am invited formerly come and *show my face*. "What is she thinking? What the hell am I supposed to say to him after all these years?" I just can't do it - but I do. As I pull up outside their gate I see him approaching with a huge smile on his face. He's still gorgeous, but then again I'm married - very married!

As we sit on the couch side by side I tell him my life's story in about ten seconds. I need him to understand that I'm married even though at this stage I would have loved to elope with him forever!
Have you ever experienced seeing someone you loved about seventeen years ago and then reconnected? It's the weirdest feeling. It's as though you want to turn back time and rectify all the mistakes that you've made and yet on the other hand it doesn't really matter. All that exists is that precious moment.

Before leaving to go to the Philippines I had gone to see a psychic called Helen. I had been to see many psychics only because I thought that they would give me some clarification of my life – none of them really seemed to assist or give me some magical formula that I so yearned for - and in the end I discovered I still had to go through my *own* life's journey. Helen on the other hand was a little different. She kind of freaked me out. She told me I would meet a

33

man with blue eyes that I already knew. This man was born in another country and worked with computers. She picked up that I was not happy in my marriage and was adamant that I would not stay married to him for longer than nine months. This gave me the challenge to prove her wrong! It had been over a year since I had seen her and therefore my proof that they were all fakes became yet again fact. To me they were all just another one of those crazy messed up weirdos looking to rip some searching soul out his or her last buck.

I was still married and now sitting next to a man with... "Oh my god, the most stunning blue eyes who I had known from the age of eight!" David worked as a computer programmer. He was going through some chaotic times in his relationship with this woman that he had by this time married. It was his second marriage and on its way out.

When it came for me to leave I felt like I could not say goodbye and therefore invited David to come to my cousin's birthday party that night where he could get to meet my daughter and husband.

Charles and I had a strange relationship. He was not at all the *'huggy, cuddly bunny'* type. If someone didn't know he was my husband, there would be no way they would ever have guessed we supposedly loved each other.

David and I sat around the fire that night like two reunited souls.

BEING APART

I see
Your spirit
Dancing in the leaves
I hear
Your voice
Whisper through the birds
I feel
Your body's warmth
Glowing light from the sun
I taste
Your scent
On everything
I touch.

We are always together
Even when apart
Never hidden
By space or distance
For that is all a farce.

Look into my soul
Listen to the melody
Connect to our life's source
As we embrace the inseparable
Nectar of our unity

ACT NINE

--------------- *Moving* ---------------

Moving to a town called Secunda where Charles was to assist with the nine-month contract arrived so quickly. We had to set up home again as all our furniture and belongings were left in the Philippines. Lucinda had to start a new school and I felt totally thrown off balance about leaving David behind. Why was it in life that we would have the chance to meet each other again and then move on?

I remembered how Pete and his wife had taught me to stay relaxed and try and keep my energy levels balanced. It was winter now and I sat on the floor behind a three bar electric heater, trying to teach myself to meditate.

My parents were very religious and therefore I knew nothing other than how I was taught to pray and believe that God would take care of my every need. This god wasn't doing a very good job in my marriage even though I had prayed for a sign or for healing in our marriage, it just didn't seem to work.

So here I was trying out a *new technique* - without a teacher. Lucinda was at school and Charles had left early to start his new venture. What was I thinking? Either way it didn't really matter. My breath had become calm and my eyes relaxed as I stared into the dark space behind my eyelids. A woman appeared. Her skin around her eyes were wrinkled. Her face looked so familiar. Was I

36

dreaming? Seeing her in my dreamlike state didn't bother me. I continued sitting and watched her as she turned her back toward me and showed me a wooden casket that carried a baby strapped in with leather ties. Who was she?

In my mind I asked "what is your name?"

"Martha" she replied and then disappeared from my vision.

This was how my new act of my life's journey begun.

THE JOURNEY

Immortal souls
Occupying surgical homes,
Restlessly sourcing fulfilment.

Unattached parasites,
Syphoned ticks,
Thirsting for life,
Yet never belong.

Voiceless sound,
Radiating coldness,
Like empty vessels yearning for tangibility.

Chained heart
Captured by illusion
Beats to win this game

Tearful joker
Burns his gown
Only to discover
It has no colour.

ACT TEN

--------*Touching the Light*-------

Charles was a reserved person and never desired or discussed any type of '*spirituality*'. He had been raised in an Anglican home and lived a renowned 'stable secure life'. I on the other hand was his total opposite.

Even though being raised in a Christian home - of which my father in his later years became an ordained minister - I yearned to find out as much as possible about other religions and spiritual practices. There was always this 'pull' inside me that ached to find the '*ultimate reality and soul's purpose*'.

At the age of Twenty-one I approached a Rabbi to express my desires to convert to Judaism. It took me over seven years before they would permit me to convert due to me being married to an Anglican. They could never understand my inner needs.

Nothing in my life seemed to be *normal* and this was probably why my continual search of life's purpose was so essential for me.

ACT ELEVEN

--------Seasonal Changes--------

Like the season, so too does life have its changes. Through the years we undergo many different experiences. Sometimes these changes are hard and our emotions get wrapped up in the whole affair.

Observing your own life from a distance can sometimes assist in finding the answers. When we look back and see that what we really got so caught up in, stressed out about, anxious and sometimes even became depressive about, by stepping back we will notice that all these situations eventually just follow their own paths and the river runs back into the ocean and all becomes how it was or would have been anyway.

As a mother I tend to try and perfect my daughter's life, hoping that she would not make the same mistakes that I made. I often catch myself telling her to do well at school, think about the consequences of her actions, plan ahead and visualise where her future lies etc., etc. - but even so, her path will run its own course and the challenges, hardships and choices that she has had to undergo will become a part of her own life's story.

What is it that we are all trying to accomplish? Every day we awake and habitually and go in search for 'more'. More money, more love, more this and more that. Will we as humans ever come to the point of total fulfilment? What makes us happy, is it the accumulated wealth, the perfect lover, husband or child. What is perfect, or in the end does it really matter?

There have been many philosophers, poets, and artists that have searched for the meaning of life. In their works of arts, lyrics or performances they attempt to express their findings and assumptions of their explorations of what I would term 'society's madness'. And so the show must go on and through whatever medium or manner humans attempt to venture into their minds to conclude from their experimental observations of life and the human psyche – the mission will inevitably be the same in some way or other - searching for 'truth'.

Life is not a bed of roses, nor is it one that we will live happily ever after. Many of us will keep on searching in anticipation for that "*yes, now I feel happy*" syndrome – but how long will that happiness last?

SCIENCE

Seeking endlessly

The infinite

Answers fruitlessly

Analysing,

Featuring,

Questioning,

Fanatics that seek

Minacious metaphors,

in space and matter.

Never cease to

Forfeit phantoms

That conquer their minds

41

ACT TWELVE

----*The Cinderella Syndrome*----

The following article was written by Fritz-Laure Dubuisson.

- Dennett's idea of universal acid can be found in many facets of human development.
Darwin's universal acid was released into the scientific world as other forms of acid were being released and eating away at foundations society had taken centuries to set up. With the foundation quickly crumbling it became the task of several self-selected individuals to patch up the cracks that were quickly becoming giant holes. Universal acid is an idea or thought that has the potential power of disintegrating long held beliefs or truths. " Darwin's idea cuts much deeper into the fabric of our most fundamental beliefs than many of its sophisticated apologists have yet admitted, even to themselves" (Dennett 18). But it can also be an idea which has the means of moulding societal norms through its mere existence.
An example of this would be fairy tales especially those written by The Brothers Grimm. These stories were not treated as a lethal form of universal acid because they were used to create social norms. In the fairy tales little girls and boys learned how to be women and men. They were also taught the rules of engagement for this new and diverse wilderness called civilization. The fairy tales and other such stories transcended culture and language. All over the world there are variations of Cinderella and other popular fairy tales.

The universal acid in these stories was used as a means for eradicating inappropriate or deviant behaviour. The acid shaped and moulded what made good little girls and boys. Those who were outside the parameters set by these stories would, according to the fairy tales themselves, meet with horrible consciences. They would either not be chosen by the prince or would not receive the award that awaited the good girl. This is displayed in Grimm's rendition of Cinderella's dying mother's words "Dear child, be good and pious, and then the good God will always protect you, and I will look down on you from heaven and be near you" (Grimm 121).

Being good is never enough. In order to survive happily in the new wilderness and individual would have to be not only good, but pretty. Beautiful, would be preferred, but being just pretty could be utilized to the individual's and their family's advantage. Through these fairy tales beauty is equated with meekness and even temperedness. These things are then used as commodities to bartered the family's way up the societal ladder and therefore increase their chances of survival in civilization.

Through the attainment of financial security the family can not only survive, but can participate in the "happily ever after" ending, if and only if they were also "good". The idea of what is "good" is also clearly described in the "stories". Being "good" means, the poor know their place; the rich are all good looking and therefore deserving of their wealth. But if by some freak chance of nature or magic, usually in the form of a fairy godmother, a "good" poor couple should happen to have an attractive child, then that child is also given access to the world of the rich.

This access is usually in the form of marriage. The poor, but good young man marries a princess after saving her from whatever situation is preventing her from being with a rich prince. The pretty and good young woman marries the prince after she has proven her ability to withstand pain, humiliation and other sorts of character building exercise. These obstacles are undoubtedly placed in her path to prepare her for a life of deserved luxury. Deserved luxury is very different for boys and girls in these long revered classics. Boys earn their right to luxury by being brave, sometimes handsome, but most defiantly steadfast and brave of heart. Girls have to be good and meek, while inspiring acts of bravery from the young men of equal or opposite economic class. As stated in the article by Marica Lieberman, "Good, poor, and pretty girls always win rich and handsome princes, never merely handsome, good, but poor men"(386).

The beauty described in these stories is very specific, just as there are certain undeniable character requirements of being "good", there are certain requirements which are made for being "beautiful". These specifications are usually set up in opposition to the female villainess in the fairy tale. If the villainess is not old and ugly then she is terribly beautiful. If she's not good and beautiful then she must be terribly beautiful or dark and beautiful. The beautiful villainess is never, merely pretty or slightly attractive, she is the ultimate beauty gone wrong. It is through her villainy that she will lose her right to not only be rich, but beautiful.
Just Cinderella's evil step-mother and step-sisters," And thus, for their wickedness they were punished with blindness all their days" (Grimm 128). The stories usually end with her disfigurement or transformation into the hideous beast within, as in Disney's rendition of Sleeping Beauty. She is the warning held up to the pretty and beautiful young women who do get the prince. Not only do they have to be "good" not, but they have to remain that way in order to keep the prince the kingdom and her looks, sometimes her life. " Among

other things, these tales present a picture of sexual roles, behaviour and psychology, and a way of predicting outcome or fate according to sex, which is important to because of the intense interest that children take in "endings"; they always want to know how things will "turn out" (Lieberman 384).

Colouring and colour also play an important role in these fairy tales, the villainess can be fair and pale to dark and dangerously beautiful. The heroine is not allowed such colour variances. She can be fair or fairer. The only things which can actually change are her hair colour or in some instance the colour of her dress. But even this usually carries countless cultural affiliations with colours that signify beauty and purity. The idea of fair can be in relation to her temperament or a direct description of her physical colouring. This interplay between colours is explicitly used in many latter works which follow the fairy tale plot, such as Comedy: American Style. Poor pretty girl, treated badly by _____, saved by equally pale or golden tanned handsome prince, after many trials and tribulations. The tan coming from his many adventures into the wilds of fairy tale land and the sun exposure he endured to come to her rescue, not biology. "Olivia dreams he light skinned daughter Teresa marries a princely (white, rich) husband. The achievement of Olivia's dream is thwarted by the larger, racial issue which informs the novel, the issue of passing"(Lupton 410).

With this new form or socially constructed natural selection, the evolution of the fairy tale story becomes a mutant. The majority of the society which the stories were meant to influence does not fulfil the Beauty category with satisfaction. It is easier for the men to fill the requirements of prince-hood, or its close relation, good and hard working. But with so many variance in the real world of the fairy tales it becomes questionable whether the existence of these stories is

45

evolutionary in their ability to shape children's minds or de-evolutionary because the checklist for hero and heroine seem so unattainable. As a form of universal acid, authors have tried to cover and recover the endings of the original Grimm's Fairy Tales, which were not all happy. The endings were being good did not necessarily save an individual for the bad things and monsters of the world. The need to attach happy endings to these stories is an admittance of the unattainable prototype.

So to make being good and pretty desirable, the happy endings were added to sooth the wounds inflicted by the ideas being carried out through the unpleasant endings of the stories. Not only could you not be happy if you weren't beautiful and good but even then, happiness is not assured. Just as Dennett include a section titled, "The Moral First Aid Manual", the happy endings were meant to act as a salve. "At every stage in the tumultuous controversies that have accompanied the evolution of Darwin's dangerous idea, there has been a defiance born of fear" (Dennett 521). This is the same fear which birthed a need to end the fairy tales happily. In the end it was not the children who could not handle having a "happily ever after", but the adults. By experiencing a world in which they did not and were not experiencing the happily ever after they needed to be able to read the fairy tales to save them from the world which was too much like world portrayed by Grimm.

After all our brainwashing of how to be the perfect Cinderella and face life, how then do we stand up and confront the world and say "I did it my way!" From the time girls can barely read, their minds are ingrained with this tale of the prince who rescues the fair maiden and whisks her away to never-never-land where overwhelming paradise prevails and they live "happily ever after." Why didn't the story include the countless heartaches good girls such as Cinderbella meet on the road to discovering Prince Charming. The numerous dates that never worked out, the guys who walked, because Cinderbella wouldn't put out, and better still, the men who had the audacity not even to show up to take the fair maiden out.

We can live in our solemn state of mental and emotional misery and try and figure out where we went wrong, why we went wrong or alternatively - move on. Making the decision to leave the past behind and concentrate our energies into what we are Now, most often has a far higher, positive impact on our personal well-being and therefore become a foundation of a well-established life - now and in our future.

Even today as I write this book I am continually reminded of my emotional attachments to my past. After almost eleven years of being divorced from Charles we still share the same interest - the interest of our daughter which is moulded into our sub consciousness and created a thought pattern that 'ticks to the same *tune*'.

Waking up this morning and having programmed myself to believe that every day is a new beginning; I prepare my mind mentally to face whatever situation decides to unfold. Oh goodness so much for self-help and positive aspirations – this day has been scripted out to be another one of those an 'unanticipated events'. Charles calls me to inform me that he wishes to leave South Africa and take on a new Golf Design project in China. My immediate reaction is to think 'wow, what an amazing opportunity!' By this time of our 'play' he has become a good friend of mine and through time - in our case - we learnt that being friends had more benefits than being the husband and wife disaster of our past.

We chat for a long time and then all of a sudden the realities hit me. Cinderbella, this Cinderbella the now independent, positive, motivated, structured, and untouchable Cinderbella, breaks down and cries. In that moment of time I experience becoming true to my own feelings. The feelings were not of sadness or regret or even insecurity, just true feelings that our sub-consciousness stores and never realises. Whether through choice or chemistry, only psychologists might be able to give the logical explanation to that, but for me I realised that somewhere through all the dilemmas of life's journeys and lessons, the true spark of love never really ever leaves your soul. I acknowledged it and came to the recognition that no matter how much we bitch or complain about our ex-husbands, ex-lovers, fathers uncles or brothers, deep down inside we store the love that we once had and held onto, hoping that in the end it really all would end up being 'happily ever after'.

The way I handle my emotions might be the same or different to the way you handle yours but in a situation like this I allow myself time. Time to think - time to get in touch with my own internal emotions – time to see, feel, hear, taste and touch them - and then time to analyse them.

Letting go is probably one of the hardest things to do. Through the year, even though it is only April, I have been confronted with numerous situations that have involved letting go in many different forms. Knowing that my daughter will be completing her final year and then probably leaving home, making decisions on whether to take on the Directorship in a new province for our eight year established Production Company, and now a new one of letting Charles go.

I walk around the garden, breathing in the fresh autumn air.

Is life really real? Is this not just an altered state of *being*? Are we playing a part in the drama of life, which has probably been rehearsed over and over again before we even entered it or is there more?

And so once again I decide that after I've let all the thoughts and philosophies blow themselves out of my mind – the rest in the end doesn't really matter!

So being who I am – the one that does not really know how to ;say what she really feels' - I decide to write the following email to Charles knowing that it will be more true to my own personality than having to speak words of 'non-substance'.

"Hi Charles,

OK got all the emotions behind me and done some logical thinking about your new venture :).

Yes, it's always hard dealing with the emotional side, because you tend to want to hold on to what you know. It's rough going to a new country, we should know and my only concern about you going is the loneliness of being there on your own. It's a wonderful opportunity and financially a good venture. You have two options, in my opinion, 1st one you don't go and carry on like you have been for the past couple of years. This is not a bad situation and it is pretty balanced because you are well established and happy. It's not that you don't have work in SA and it can grow but probably take more time than if you had to go overseas. It is always nice knowing that you are there for us even though it's a phone call away :).

2nd option you go overseas. If you do decide on this it will take a lot of sacrificing. 1. Your country that you know, missing your friends and family. Can you handle the loneliness? Sometimes I wish that Tracey would be more supportive and maybe consider going with you, I would have :)!

49

Knowing your personality like I do I think that I would encourage option 2... Why? .... You are a high power driven person, who loves new challenges. You survived Swaziland, which is about as isolated as China! Your life at the moment is pretty isolated when you do your various projects all over SA. The only difference is that you are in a country that you know.

When we moved to Philippines we were excited about going and would have probably stayed there for as long as it took, had the project taken off. You felt good about going, even so that we were prepared to sell up the home, which was an extra emotional thing, but we went! It was great and taught us so much about life. it was only a matter of jumping on the plane and coming back home if we wanted to, whenever we wanted to. In those days even that amount we were paid in dollars gave us the extra bit of freedom that it takes to do things in life.

I know that you are probably feeling like there's too many sacrifices involved in going to China, which obviously there are, but if you do decide to go I know that it will be greatly rewarding for you in the long run. Being like you are, and if you turned down the opportunity, you would feel defeated and maybe in the long run even regret it.

Whatever decision you make, know that I will support it.

If you do go, then have the right purpose behind it. Do it for Lucinda and maybe you will have a positive attitude? So many people out there in life have no purpose, no kids no nothing. You and I are the type of people that need to have a purpose to make us wake up in the morning and say "I can, I will, and I want to!"

If you make up your mind to go then live with that in mind, and if you decide not to go, then have a reason and a purpose behind that too. Either way, you are amazing and even if you didn't make another cent in your life, Lucinda and I would still love you and ALWAYS be proud of YOU...

50

Take your time and know that your decision will be the right one, because it's your life!

You are responsible for your own happiness through the choices and decisions that you make as long as you have u ***reason and purpose behind them****!*

ACT TEN

--- *Feels Like Yesterday.* ---

It feels like yesterday that David and I sat around the fire and discussed our lives of being apart. As we interacted and exchanged our stories of happiness and failures we could both sense that there was still a huge connection between the two of us even after all these many separated years. But time had moved on - too quickly you may say, but in this case it had left us in a situation that being adult meant being responsible and being responsible was the solution to our long lost love. I could have done the most irresponsible act that night and eloped to '*forever- forever land*' with David - but I didn't and I couldn't - I had to be responsible!

Being a responsible mother, wife and adult was what I had been programmed to be and become. Society to me was the most 'stuffed-up' theory but going against the masses sometimes had a lot of challenging detriments. Time alone would *tell* the tale but for that moment all we could do was enjoy the moment of our reunion.

Lucinda was only five years old. She was a *happy go lucky* type of child and nothing ever got her down. By this early age she had already lived in Asia and experienced the different cultures that our world had to offer. Charles and I never really followed any particular religion and therefore Lucinda grew up having an open mind to life, politics and religion – this for us I can say through times grace has showed its benefits. Now at almost eighteen, she embraces life in an un-judgmental manner, accepts people for who they are no matter what their colour, creed or belief system may be.

We as humans have this strange conception that we can arrange our lives to fit into little categories and label them under 'unique' headings. Some of these labels may read 'perfect', 'right', 'wrong', 'try harder', 'eat less', 'take control', 'submit', 'wife', 'mother', 'failure', 'success' and many thousands of more *titles* that we give to items and icons so as to continuously remind ourselves of how we should 'fit in' or 'lose out'. We have a tendency to strive and perfect our *roles* as we *play the game of life*. There have been hundreds of best seller titles that give us *'unique, individuals'* new hopes to fulfil our destinies and yet by doing so, so often tend to categorise us as one of Hitler's perfect race rather than giving us the opportunity to exploit our own uniqueness. I'm not saying that all theories are harmful but rather trying to give you the option of maybe 'stepping back' and analysing *who* you are rather than falling into a *systematically society* syndrome. How will you cope if your perfect little categorised 'marriage' just happens to fall apart or your 'stable teenager' decides to go off the rails? Knowing who you are, really truly believing that you are unique and accepting it, will often give you enough drive and encouragement to make the right decisions in any situation.

It's a hard path to follow and not many out there right now will even attempt to 'step off' their 'luxurious pedestals' and have the guts to experiment with a proposition such as *'Learn to find who you are'* type of statement. It does take courage and yes sometimes the structured walls will collapse - but building a 'new foundation' rather than the one that you have sweated and not completely understood anyway, can more times than often become the root and start of a complete fulfilment in your life.

In June 1997 I decided to take the challenge. Walking out of our apartment, I took the decision to *follow my heart*. At this stage of my journey I knew no better than to leave what I no longer felt passionate about. I had gone through the *near death experiences* when I faced my terminal illness and had vowed to myself that I would never stay in a situation that caused me to 'eat myself up'. With two hundred and fifty Rand in my purse I 'walked out' - leaving all my worldly possessions behind. I had no direction or even a structured game-plan of where I was going or what I would do, but enough determination that I had to be true to myself. Poetry was a means that I could interact with my sub- consciousness and with the three poems in my mind that I receipted as they were nursery rhymes – switch on my car ignition and headed into a direction that my heart was aching for - to find the person I had lost.

TIMELESS MEMORIES

Whispering words of madness,
Silencing the acid air
With memories enclosed in a web of mind
As they subtly dispose their fears.
Noughts and crosses,
Snakes and dice,
Race to tie the knot
Of timeless memories.

EMBRIO

Hands clutched
Eyes closed
Captured in a womb
Attached to a cord
Dependent on woman
Exposed to vibrations
Fed no choice
Imprisoned.

Escape my innocence,
Open my blindness.
Free my space,
Cut me loose.
Give me independence,
Unexposed to fear,
Feed me love,
Eternally.

ACT FOURTEEN

--- *Into the Darkness to Find The Light.* ---

Stepping into this irrational choice made me feel a little uncomfortable. I had stepped out of my 'comfort zone' into a bizarre unstructured situation. Arriving at my aunt's farm I felt rather inferior. It felt as though I was invading another woman's domain. My cottage that they offered me would serve as a retreat hive. Here I would spend time isolating myself and try and come to terms with what I wanted and why. I was away from my daily responsibilities of having to play 'mother', 'wife' and 'dying soul'. This would be a time for 'me' - but who was 'I'?

By the time I had left Charles we had signed the papers and agreed that our relationship was dead, even so I knew that he did not really accept the fact that it might be for real. There had been no arguing or discrepancies over the decision. I had approached our family lawyer, paid the deposit into his account, and signed the contract - and now a few days later - sat in a minute cottage and totally detached from all of life's expectations. What would I be confronted with next? – These and many other adventures were soon to follow.

How often do we find ourselves trying to pre-plan our lives? It's true that goal setting have their positive attributes as well as negative

56

implications - but I'm talking about 'living too much in our future and missing out on the present sunlight'. Three years ago when I decided that I wanted to write a book called "when Cinderbella gets divorced", it was going to be about how woman must take control of their lives, fight until death and suck men out of anything they could possibly get! It would have been based on my own anger, fears and hurts of my own mistakes. Through time I have been given the privilege of understanding the meaning of life in a different manner. Writing this book I personally experience the healing and love that can come from any lesson that I underwent each new day and therefore write a *new chapter* in a unplanned way, allowing the universe to give me events that can make me a stronger person and heal not only me but encourage you the reader to become a witness of your own healing process.

I remember sitting outside our school hall while waiting for the school bus to arrive. We had been writing our final matriculation examinations and had a few extra hours to pass before the younger grades were dismissed. As I sat in my 'dream state' I watched the ants working. It was so fascinating to see them scurrying along with complete awareness of their individual mission. They even seemed to stop and have time for a chat. Such small creatures yet completely aware of their daily purpose, whether or not they got to ever lay eyes on the queen ant or not, they just happily continued performing their duties. It's their attitude. If they became miserable and complained about every nana particle they had to lift each day or about how they never got the expected reward for their daily task, would they ever keep up the team spirit?

How often do we miss out on the small details of life? So often we get caught up in our whole drama and miss out on the simplicities and beauties of life. When you are sitting watching these small insects it becomes as though you for a few minutes are playing god.

And yes we can. We, in life, have the right to choose. God gave us a brain - let's use it. We don't have to be structural human beings that function robotically day in and day out. We can have a little chat along the way - we can show compassion and love, - and best of all, we are allowed to! There's an old Jewish saying that says "*God helps those that help themselves*". Isn't this so true to life?

We are responsible for our own happiness. There will be times that life throws some unexpected event onto our laps, and yes they might not always be so pleasant, but how we help ourselves during these testing times are determines the outcome. Many times I think even God must have a smile on his face and most probably thinks to himself "Goodness, having them change their attitude sure takes the load of my shoulder!"

LIGHT

Creatures of darkness
Snuck silently in oneness
Eyes tensed tightly
As they huddle united
In their privileged
Pride of prejudice.

No mercy murmured their minds
As they fought fiercely
For what was theirs
They were sucklings of sinners
And then
Oh then .....
God said,
Let there be light!

------ What's the Meaning of Happiness? ------

As a woman I find that we tend to have different needs than men. Is it possible for them to ever figure us out completely? Every new day brings new challenges but for me it also seems to bring new desires and dreams.

David, who being the logical one of us two, can never really figure me out and as sure as hell I don't blame him!

As we grow older our needs change. We yearn for love in a different *form*. We want to believe that we can trust and be trusted, love and be loved. To me it is a yearning for 'real' love.

If there was one product I could buy of the shelf it would be 'unconditional love'. There has been so much hype about the definition of unconditional love but even so it all boils down to a love with no expectations. It's a love that gives without needing to be rewarded or appraised for any reason. We all search for that perfect lover, husband, or friend but coming into contact with finding 'unconditional love' inside ourselves is like finding a friend forever.

There have been many Masters, Gurus and Saints that have talked about the concept of 'unconditional love'. Christ explains that the kingdom of heaven is within you. What does this mean? We run around each day trying to find pleasures in many different forms, and sometimes they might even give us temporary satisfaction. The question is, does it last? Getting a high from purchasing that beautiful, black BMW; will it last? Flying overseas and staying in the finest hotels and dining out each night on the most ravishing extravagant foods and wine; how long will it be before the novelty wears off and the yearning for something more, something better and something newer cries out from inside our ever searching minds?

A dear friend of mine, a woman that has been a single mother after getting divorced twelve years ago, calls me up to tell me that she has a really hectic meeting. She has borrowed a man fifty thousand rand a few months ago. It is not money that she can spare but rather money that has come from the profit of her town house that she had sold. Ann is a book keeper and has to works hard to earn the pennies for her monthly living expenses.

Arriving at one of her clients she finds him in tears. He is taking strain in business and she being the kind-hearted person that she is, holds him and in the spare of this emotional moment decides that she will lend him the money. Lending him the money is done through love but now many months down the line, the grateful man has turned his back on the re payment commitment - and the once 'out of love' situation has become a warfare.

What does a woman do in a situation like this, does she pick up the phone and speak to the most brutal attorney and leave it all up to them to sort the matter out or does she follow her instincts and leave it up to a higher power? I have learnt in life that different situations need different approaches. Knowing Ann like I do, I agree that we will do it the 'magical' way. She is wearing her purple shirt, a very influential colour. I am some thirty kilometres away from her but even so I know that distance does not count. She is nervous and like most woman, not ready to get into any type of confrontational situation. Lighting my candles and incense in my meditation room I focus on her intent and in spirit we agree upon the situation. You can

61

call it a 'magical working' or any other term you wish, but the bottom line it is a working that in faith the situation will work out for the good of all and harm non. Drawing out an inspirational card on Ann's behalf, I silently read the affirmation "I can risk doing what I feel is right".

Half an hour later she calls. I am expecting a positive outcome but the universe knows the bigger picture and why some situation don't always turn out to be like we think they will. He has pleaded poverty and cannot say when he can repay his debt.

Now you are probably thinking "the idiot, sue him". It's not always quite that simple, and when you have left a situation up to the universe, then that is what you do.

There have been many lessons that have come from a single situation like this. For one, Ann has learnt to confront her fears by approaching her client. She knows that after all these months of politely asking and begging him to repay her, nothing has come from it. Now the 'letting go' and having the confidence enough to confront him personally had allowed her to become a 'stronger' woman than she had been a few hours before.

We are all put onto this planet to learn and grow in different ways. Your fears might not be the same as mine and vice versa, but by letting go of our *egos* we allow ourselves to become more and more in touch with *who* we really are. We are not just out here to be pathetic little human beings - we are powerful immortal souls and part of the universal energies. How beautiful it is when we begin to grasp that we are a part of the whole 'big picture'. We can make a difference to the whole well-being of this planet even if it's by doing just a tiny good deed. Changing our attitudes and circumstances, from a once negative into a positive approach has timelessly been proven to make an impact and a difference to the outcome. Isn't that amazing! Ann has changed her attitude from one that was negative and angry to one that is positive and powerful. She has put her faith in a higher *source* than herself and through that small change I do believe that the situation will be taken care of in its own time in a much more beautiful way.

I've always firmly believed that when praying or asking for a higher power to assist us it is useful to include a sentence that indicates, for instance, *'that it is for the good of all and that it harms none"*. This allows for positive energies to play their roles and take care of the situation in the correct manner. There is already so much hatred, wars, poverty and crime in our country and therefore trying to play God is not what should be done if done in purity and love. It is far greater to leave it up to Him/her as that is what we are asking for – for assistance to make the right choice, be guided etc., etc. Thereafter I believe we should act in faith and become intuitive to which doors open or close. Learning to follow what you believe is correct and taking the risk to do what is right, allows for rapid change and healing in all situations.

I remember writing a poem to Charles a few years before I left him.

TO MY LOVE

You just don't understand
Why I feel like I do,
I need to be me,
I need to be myself,
I've been so like everyone,
For so very long,

Please understand just this once,
It's not that I don't want you,
To have anything you want too,

63

I only want to set myself free,
To be me,
Only for a while!

It sounds like I'm saying "I",
But it's important to ME.
"I" need to be the unique,
"I need to plat MY hair,
"I" need to run bare foot,
"I" need to be ME,
Please!
Only for a while!

Women, I feel, long to have their partners understand them. Many partners find them too complex, but yes that's what makes us unique *beings*. Being an artist and author makes me unique. I have my moody days and I have my bubbly ones but that doesn't mean that I can be put into a little box and labelled '*Artist*'. Yes I agree there are many other similar artists that are temperamental but I like to see myself as being unique. Today I might want my hair coloured purple and tomorrow it might just need to be green - but so what - as long as I am not running around trying to get satisfaction from an unsatisfying source - Who cares? We are allowed to change. We are allowed to be *unique beings* and even more so, we are allowed to be who we really are and love it!

Being happy is what every person strives for. In South Africa through the years of apartheid Blacks were put under incredible suppression. Now many years later, in our democratic country, they have been given the freedom to be who they really are and always were. Isn't that the same in life where we put ourselves under the rules of society and conform to their ideals? All we are doing is suppressing our *true* selves. I'm not saying go against the countries rules, but basically just trying to allow you to see that you have the freedom to be who you really are. Just because you are a wife doesn't mean you can't dance in the moonlight or walk around with a smile. You wonder why South Africa has one of the highest divorce rates in the world, maybe it's because partners are getting so sick and tired of seeing each other's miserable faces. How do you think your husband or wife, boyfriend or girlfriend would react if the next time they came home or saw you and you had a smile on your face? Put yourself in the reverse, how would you react if your partner or friend looked happy? That's the difference, we can make the difference. We are allowed to make the world a happier place. Whatever situation arises we have full permission to change our attitudes and become in touch with who we really are – complete, whole, full of light and love.

It is the most frustrating situation in life when the "honeymoon" stage wears off. It's wonderful being '*in love*' and being told how you make each other have a reason to be alive. Remember the first time you lay eyes on each other or the first kiss; it was more than likely the most amazing moment. One that you wish you could capture and save in a bottle for a few years down the line when things by this stage have probably become stale. How do we cope with the staleness? That's when the *cravings* for something better - something bigger - or something more, start creeping in. But in the end after three, four, five or six marriages/relationships down the line, will it be enough or perfect? The answer is "no". There is no perfect partner that will be the *perfect partner for life*, so get over it. What I feel that we are really searching for is to be in love with our *self* and have peace within.

I must say that having a partner that supports your ideas is a hell of a lot easier than having one that runs you down all the time. The latter situation would more than likely mean that this is the lesson you have chosen in your life. How will you face this negative partner? Will you keep submitting because of fear? Fear of failure, fear of rejection and more times than most 'fear of *Self*'.

When things just really don't work out and you've tried every shrink, prayed to every moon, prayed to the ants and prayed to every possible moving or unseen *being*, you may start to wonder if this *Cinderbella* will ever believe or trust again. It is always great having happy memorable occasions, but what when the *bubble* cracks? Will you question yourself deeply in order to believe that it is really all over?

Going through my divorce with Charles was when I wondered how I could have been so stupid to ever believe in all the fantasies and lies that I had been indoctrinated with by 'Grimm'.

LIES

'til death do us depart,
I surrender my all,
To love and to hold you,
To answer to your call.

We will never leave,
What we've joined together,
Hurt or hardships,
We will last forever.

Rings were symbolic,
As a token of eternity,
Jurisdictions now remind me,
Of our lies of purity.

nly time has taught me that the lessons that I had chosen were for my *own* benefit. Now looking back I have learnt to accept and realise that going through the lesson of getting divorced have become my *gift* only because I started to learn to *let go*. To let go of the anger, the blaming, the regrets, and *accept* that out of the negative situation there came light. I stopped blaming God for not giving me what I had asked and prayed for and accepted that the eventual outcome would be for the best of us all because of His will for my life.

ACT SIXTEEN

-- To Divorce or not to Divorce? --

THE FOOL

Tears flow like vinegar
as the mascara helps hide my skin
Where is the one I believed in,
or is it truly me that has changed our course?

Love does not exist
I'm beginning to learn that fast
It lasts momentarily,
then vanishes back to its source
Oh it's me that has changed
I should have known that through remorse!

Hugs strangle me
Kisses shut my mouth
Words deafen my ears
Lies engulf my pain

Love, life and longevity
Fade fast the words so faked.

While trying to fathom out what it was that I was searching for, yet becoming quite content with my choice of staying in my aunts little cottage while I allowed myself to work it out, I had time to play.
Playing is one of the first gifts that we tend to give up when we get married.
As children we live each day playing.

Our imaginations are ripe and we become inventors of every possible fantastical game.

Then we grow up, and we use our time to seek the best possible career, make the quickest and fastest buck, buy the 'make me look thin' outfits, try every possible diet and fad so as to become 'in control' of our lives and bodies in the hope to find the perfect prince. Finding that prince is amazing, we lose our appetites, live on love and escape into our child-like imaginations once again to try and sweep him off his feet. He does the same. He knows just what to say, how to act, what tunes to play, how to enchant you to smell his love, engulf you with his desirable infatuating love and then – oh yes then my dear – he will be yours forever – all you have to do is act correctly.

David who was now living permanently with his mother after leaving his ex-wife started spending more and more time with me.

It was wonderful. I was a free woman, one that could laugh again about the most bizarre incidences. I didn't have to explain the reason for my 'madness' and if I wanted to do something bizarre - I did it! Nothing felt stressful any more. I was alive!

So this was what they meant by *'life after death'* - I had found heaven. Now God became a living creature and I started to believe that if God was a 'he' then I would rather change 'it' to be a 'she'. *This god had an imagination, it* loved pretty things, 'she' loved the sounds that nature made and sometimes even turned up the volume and danced with me.

David's and my relationship was a platonic as we had both agreed that after coming out of one disastrous relationship, who the hell would want to get involved in another!

He started teaching me how to meditate and all about how the stars out there shone because of a particular impact, about quantum physics, the properties of crystals etc., etc. He was so interesting and the world that he loved was far different to the one I knew.

As we sat watching the stars I could see the scars that the hurt he had experienced in his life had left behind – it showed by the number of lines on his face.   His hair ran down to his waist and he was gorgeous, maybe not to others but to me. Why had no one else seen the uniqueness in this man?   Why had the women that had been given the opportunity to share his life with him in the past been so unloving and forgotten how to play?

What was I thinking - I too was in a similar situation - my relationship was buried so far buried under the ground that not even an archaeologist would have been able to find it.

Looking back now, after analysing my own life, I have come to the realisation that the start of our marital problems began when I allowed myself to stop 'playing' - I will admit that yes, I too had forgotten to play! I had become a wife without an imagination. Even though I tried to always be the *good Cinderbella* and *love the prince* after he had worked and slogged it out all day, I had lost the ability to keep the candle going – you know the one that has a twinkle of adventure in it.
Electricity had replaced candles that originally accompanied the past romantic dinner table, television had become a replacement to the *Lionel Richie* songs and even more so *the flowers had died*!

The universe had pre-designed this reunion that David and I were experiencing and in my wildest imagination I could never have chosen a better *being* to help me go through my divorce than the man that was sitting next to me now - it was like magic!

My seventeen years younger sister Maryanne has always looked up to me. Even going through my divorce she is the one and only family member that I can say was there for me without having any ulterior motives.

Years later she too wants to fall into the *trap of marriage*, and find the prince.

It worried me that she hadn't learnt from my mistakes and I expressed my concerns to her in a poem. Then I began to realise that everyone has *their own right to choose*.

Naturally, being her older sister, I was being over protective and trying to live out *her* purpose in order to prevent her from getting hurt. I was trying to take on *her* lessons in life and therefore was only interfering in God and the universe's perfect will. Maryanne is a personal trainer. You know one of those cover girls that you find in the 'body' books! She has a body that any woman would die for - the *perfect Cinderbella* and a good catch" for any prince.

Early this year she married. She had always gone out with a man with a good body, the perfect '*He Man*' type of look. Meeting her now and her newlywed husband, you would have wondered if she had been taking drugs during her choice! He was the most unattractive, big-bellied man I could ever have matched her up with - even Cupid would agree - but it was *her choice* and her choices will become her own lessons.

There are so many labelled 'divorcees' that will try and tell you about their pains and sacrifices that they have had to make because of this story or that - but even so, we have to make our own choices without trying to *piggy-back* on someone else's mistakes, lessons or blessings.

How beautiful it is to make mistakes, because given time, it allows each individual to find their own strengths, weaknesses and allow them through their own willingness to either dwell in their past or accept that the circumstances at a given phase were actually blessings that encouraged personal growth. How wonderful it is when one can learn that the dark clouds have been actual God-given 'gifts'. It's your choice how you want to see them. Learning how to focus on the *positive* aspects of any situation will help you find that it wasn't really '*real*' anyway, and that the monster behind the curtain in fact was only a shadow created by the moon – a distorted misconception of your actual true '*self*'.

OH TO BE WED.

The prince never arrives
On that white horse
The toad
Never turned
into what was said
to be wed
is that of fairy tales off course.

Run maiden hide
Your little prince
Is dead.

Brides laden
in heavy white gowns
their future is harmonious
so they are told
life from this day
will offer them only

hardships and frowns.

Run maiden hide
Or your heart
Will turn cold.

They whisper sweet
I love you forever
Your ears
Are clogged by wax
Stay by your side
And leave you never
Run maiden hide
Where you can then relax.

-　　　　Written for my sister Maryanne

ACT SEVENTEEN

--------*Thief in the Night*------

There is much excitement in South Africa today.

Word has it that Baba Ji, one of the Eastern Philosophy Masters, has arrived in Johannesburg. Cell phones ring from early hours of the morning as animated followers spread the word. The connections are made. His supporters as well as seekers make hasty and eager preparations to go meet their Master.

Isn't it so outlandish how humans are - they crave to belong; they desire to feel secure - but are they prepared to make the sacrifices?

I remember my father preaching about how Jesus would come back to fetch his followers and arrive like a thief in the night. It used to make me feel terrified and I wondered if this ghost-like figure would remember to locate me amongst all the billions of other people on this planet or would I be left behind? As I grew older I began to comprehend this allegory. It became almost symbolic of how I should live my life being true to myself. It meant walking a path that no matter what situation arrived I would always know that what I was doing was justifiable. I have analysed so many different faiths and watched how they act out their 'holier than thou' parts in their places of worship but once away and behind closed doors the *costumes fall*s and the fox that hid in the sheep's clothing shows his true self. I'm not saying I'm perfect and yes we are all human but I do feel that if you are going to follow a particular faith, path, philosophy, culture or creed - at least try practising what you preach.

How many women have you seen that let themselves go after only a few months down the line of getting married? They start taking on that *I'm married now forever* type of appearance and become fat nagging housewives with miserable frowns.

Personally I have found that by taking pride in myself not only makes me feel and look good, but also gives me the confidence to take on the attitude that I will 'never surrender to what I believe is best for me'. *He might just come as a thief in the night and you should always be ready.* You have no guarantee that your relationship will last forever, nor can you live in fear about it, but by putting your best into the present relationship sure helps it last that extra day.

Try this simple experiment and pretend that today is the first day in your present relationship. How will you change what you usually do when you wake up in the morning?

It's not always easy I know and I remember teaching the students at one of my meditation classes how they should try and do this little ritual – I'd say "Go into the bathroom. Look yourself in the mirror and say to yourself "I love you". It stirs many different emotions that we so often have covered up so deep down inside ourselves. By doing this we will experience that in actual fact we might even have stopped loving ourselves. Once we can start loving the "I" again, we can become in love with the "me". It gives us a new sense of why we want to take care of ourselves, because we love the 'I'. This does not mean that you have to walk around with the biggest ego or go on the quickest and latest fad diet; it just means that by becoming *in touch* with the person you forgot about or lost, is given a new chance to feel alive and loved again.

Each one of us is unique, we are special and that uniqueness is what makes us precious co-creators of this enormous universe. We can

75

choose to become like one of the stars that shine in the darkness of the night or alternatively just remain in our own misery and cover our light under a bushel – it's our choice.

We all have our own stories of the hardships that we might have gone through but moving on and seeing the beauty in that lesson is what makes us expand and accept our own self-worth.

Change can be a frightening word for many people.
There are so many seminars, books and philosophies that encourage you to change. I don't like the concept and have found that accepting who I am *right now* has a far more positive outcome than one that would tell me to change. Accepting myself in this present moment, this day, this minute, this place creates a sense of security within me. It helps me get in touch with who I am and *'love it'*. This has helped me through times of stressful times and I recall the moment when Charles lay on the floor in the early hours of the morning having gone through a mild stroke just hours before he was to compete in the Sun City Golf Tournament. At that present moment I had to be in touch with myself. It would not have helped if I had become too frightened, too insecure, too pathetic or worried about the final outcome. Getting Charles to a hospital that was more than ninety kilometres away was all that was important. Divorcing him seven years later presented me with a completely different yet similar scenario, one in which I had to become *in touch with myself* and *live each day for its present moment in time*. This helped me to let go of the past and love each day for what it had to offer knowing that I would always be guided and looked after as long as I was *true to myself.*

SUBSTATION

Trying to pretend

You're not so insecure

Makes it oh so obvious

That you're not that happy after all

You analyse

Criticise,

Mesmerise,

Pathetic hypocritical victim.

Grasp your situation

Find that match that sparks

the truth of your resurrection.

--- *What Woman Want?* ---

The answer to *what woman want* has been debated by many a man and women and I am not quite sure if anyone has totally figured out the factual conclusion or if they are still being classified as *assumptions* or stored in the *to be continued* articles One of the stories that so beautifully described this was one that was told to me by my dear friend Ann.

It tells of how King Arthur sends out an appeal to all the knights in his kingdom. What he needs to know is the answer to *what women want*. In return King Arthur will reward the finder to the solution half of his kingdom.

The Knights enthusiastically mount their horses in quest to discover the answer. Sir Lancelot comes across an unsightly old hag in the middle of the forest. She is riddled with warts and laden with filthy rags. Politely he approaches her and says "Excuse me dear madam, I am in search of an answer to King Arthur's request. Will you be as kind as to allow me a few moments of your time?" The hag smiles and invites him into her cottage. His eyes chase tensely around this old woman's eerie cabin. From the ceiling hang rat's tails and unimaginable possessions and he wonders to himself if he will ever live to tell the story. She offers him warm butternut soup. As he looks into her eyes he can tell that behind this ugly creature there is a heart that is kind and gentle. He relaxes and begins to ask her "Sweet, generous and loving lady, would you perhaps know the answer to what woman want?" The hag sniggers and replies,

"Indeed I do but before I can depart with my great wisdom you will have to prove you are honourable. First you must agree to spend the night with me in my cabin, and after we are wed it will be revealed". Sir Lancelot ponders the provocation and realises that he has nothing to lose except the fact that he might land up being married to an old ugly woman who probably doesn't have much longer to live anyway. He agrees.

After spending the night with this old crone he keeps his promise and returns to his town and marries. On their honeymoon night she asks him "Oh handsome love, if you could choose between having me beautiful at night where I would fulfil your every sexual fantasy and bestow you your hearts desires or beautiful in the day where all your friends would lay eyes on me and be envious of the woman you have wed, what would you choose?"

Sir Lancelot smiles at his bride and answers "I would allow you to choose". With a great flash of light the once ugly old wife becomes the most ravishing and gorgeous woman he has ever laid his eyes upon and she remains that beautiful woman for the rest of her life.

Sir Lancelot has discovered the answer to King Arthur's question. The moral of the story is that what women want *is the freedom to choose*.

So often once two people have committed themselves to marriage they land up feeling more and more claustrophobic.

I have this *thing* about wanting to keep my own *identity*. Just because I'm married does not mean that I have to act and behave like "Mrs Jones".

In my last marriage I landed up having to sacrifice who *I really was* and this caused me to become ill. I say *I landed up having to* but in actual fact it was my *choice*. I didn't *have to do* anything. I allowed myself to fall into this trap and therefore had to take the consequences. Because of my past experience I am more adamant about never allowing myself to go through a situation again that may cause me to lose my own sense of identity. It is important for me that the partner that I am with understands the boundaries. We might be a couple, sharing the same bed under the same roof but there are certain important things that I claim as my *sacred self*. Music has always been one of my passions and through the years I have collected various albums. These CD's are part of my *sacred self* and I expect other members in the house to respect this fetish. It's not wrong or right, *it just is*. Certain items allow me to have a sense of *security* that I acclaimed as my own *self-identity* and by handing over these 'weapons' I feel I could just become something I allow myself to become trapped into as I did in my previous past and lesson. Visually you could imagine two or more people living under the same roof. They are all different in some way or the other. There is no way in hell that all three of these people could be identical in every aspect of their lives. What makes them unique in my opinion is that they have their own *identities*. Whether they're fat or thin, enjoy listening to heavy rock or prefer the silence, it doesn't matter. It's their *choice*. Now by throwing all three of these people's interests and identities into a big round pot will sure cook up a good stew, but when it comes to tasting the stew you will eventually find that the ingredients might clash or match. Trying to transform this stew back to becoming the *original contents* will not be possible because everything has altered its state. The same goes for giving up everything. There has to be compromises, that I do agree, but maintaining a sense of unique identity sure can help save your sanity when you need to get back in touch with that long lost *self*.

EVICTION

Scrutinised by hypocritical prototypes.
brought to judgment
by those who detest disorder,
but clothe themselves in uniformed robotic mannerisms
while imprisoning their hypnotised desires
against truth and woeful emotions.

Piety of life has determined my fate
to love another was to discriminate
conforming is pleasurable, so I'm taught
enlightenment toward derision denounced.

Plagued by militant masters,
Vultures of fame and acceptability,
Imprisonment my fateful state is announced
Pitilessly I escape death woes
And enter into an altered consciousness
to love another
Once more

ACT NINETEEN

--------------*Trusting*--------------

One of the blessings that life has gifted me with has been to work with people in need. Having gone through my own experience of having cancer it has taught me how to become sensitive to others. Having this passion has been rewarding and during the past eleven years I have worked with people from all walks of life.

In South Africa our Black people tend to be very superstitious. Many who have illnesses would rather consult a Traditional Healer, known as a *Sangoma*. Unfortunately many of these Traditional Healers have become commercial gurus and charge astronomical fees for their services - it is very sad to see how their gifts have become less important to them than the exchange of money. Personally I have felt that if your gift becomes a money making racket, it will be taken away.

I have witnessed people that have the gift of being a natural healer, change overnight because of the *'I'* and the *'ego'* that they take on. Just by remembering that if you have been blessed with the *gift* of being able to help people believe that they will get better, you will be humble and therefore acknowledge that you are not the healer but merely the channel. You as a person – as an *'I '* and an *'ego'*, can do nothing. Yes, your positive input and projections will be necessary but the person in need will have to have the *desire* and *trust* before any noticeable improvements or healing occurs. Being aware that the *sincerity of your intentions will bring about the success of your deeds* is the starting point of all things.

A few days ago I was approached by Siphewe, a village local worker. His feet were swollen and the pain he was experiencing had become unbearable. Being as superstitious as he is, he explained to me how someone had been putting bad *'muti'* on him – this is an African term used for medicine. He was convinced that he was going to die unless I helped him. I knew that there was nothing I could do to help him, but I believed that it was possible for him to get better because of his trust in me and the work that I do. I started preparing him a bag that he was told to hang around his neck. As I collected the various herbs, stones and essential oils to accompany the *medicine pouch* - in my mind I projected an image of him becoming well again. I believed that Siphewe would become better and that because of his desire he would be a witness of the miraculous power of the universe. Two days later he phones, his voice ecstatic – he is completely healed!

It is quite easy to start taking the credit for the healing, but just as important to remember that you are not God. I remember the quote from the bible that my parents used to tell me while I was growing up which says something like – *If two or three are gathered in my name it will be done.* This always stuck in my mind as I grew up and/or followed various religious paths. No matter what religious path it was, they all had the same outlook - *where there is a will there is a way.* I have witnessed the power of prayer as well as the power of positive projections.

Leaving Charles with having as little as two hundred and fifty Rand in my pocket and having no other means of receiving money - taught me how to *survive.* I could have decided that it was easier just to surrender and stay married. This would have meant going against my heart's belief and therefore stayed on, not for the sake of love but rather comfort. I could never live that lie. My parents were distraught and disregarded my decision. They prayed anxiously, pleaded with me to reconsider what I was doing. Their prayers did not work – I did not have the desire to be with a man who I no longer loved!

TWO O' CLOCK

What am I fighting for?
Is it pain that keeps my clock ticking?
Is it for the sake of believing in nothingness,
That I wake each morn
To come back for more
Until this game is won
And the heroes die in peace
Knowing that there is no tomorrow
No truth
No life after death
Only a fantasy of yesterdays that await their next life
And yet in agony they yearn for more
Hoping that the sun will fade their desires
And that their awakening will vanquish their dreams of
Eternal love.
I surrender thee oh immortal fucked up sanity,
I forgive and forget that you ever allowed this world
To dictate to me things of what to be, how to be, what to say and
how to live.
No more she cried, it is done, I have learnt how not to live
Now set my spirit free,
to burn in hell eternally.
How could I have been so ignorant in this life?
Sold my soul to lies,
Believed in make believes'
In love that never was?
Was it denunciation of oneself that crucifixion got its name?
Forgive me father I have sinned,
Now take me yonder to undo what I have done.

ACT SEVENTEEN

--- *Moving On* ---

The first two years after leaving Charles could have been the hardest times in my life, had I allowed it. I had made the decision to move on and never surrender, no matter what!

David became my support system. He was kind and patient and allowed me the opportunity to speak. This sounds strange – speak. Have you ever felt that you just want to speak? Speak about how you're feeling, about your pains, your fears, your longings and even regrets? I did, especially during this time. In some ways I felt like my life had fallen apart, my slipper had cracked into a million pieces and even though I knew that I was doing the right thing, it still was painful! Having no support from my family and friends, I had to start a new life. I wondered how it would all land up in the end but for that time I knew I had to live each new day for what it had to offer me – I had to survive, I had to be positive.

David and I moved to Johannesburg where we both found employment. We were both down and out, he being in seven thousand Rand overdraft and me with the exceptionally small amount of money I had to my name. Charles seemed to be using this tactic of cutting off our once joint bank accounts to try and convince me that I really needed him. Even though we both knew it was over between us, he fought for his losses – me! It never makes sense why men and women that have once been in love, had children together, worked and struggled to make a success in their lives etc., had to always fight and cause each other so much pain the minute it didn't work out the way it did in Grimm's Fairy Tales. Why couldn't they just part and go their own separate ways and *live happily ever after*? Either way it was something that I had to stand by. My decision had been made!

The tiny cottage that we rented became my new home. It was different from the homes I had lived in the past – but it was 'home'.
I thanked the *Great Spirit* above each day for looking after me and for giving me a roof over my head.
It was wonderful to be in a new space that I could feel the warmth and love that David and I shared. After a very long time I was now able to be myself again. The bells that hung off the doors and windows, the Oriental cloths that glowed, the smell of incense and vegetable curry that flowed throughout the cottage - reminded me of how I used to be – the *me* I had lost, the *self* that I had allowed to be change by submitting to Charles's expectations. I was free!
My mother had warned me that I would *land up in the gutters* if I left my comforts and divorced Charles. I was determined that I would survive and prove them all wrong! It wasn't as though I was playing a game - if it was it would probably have not felt real. What I was going through and experiencing every day was very much real! Well I thought it was until I started reading the book called *"A Course in Miracles"*. This book *blew my brains*. It seemed to come into my life at the perfect time and helped me to understand that it wasn't real, that in fact life is/was an illusion. I fought this concept and challenged the universe. I found myself spending more and more time focusing on the present, meditating and asking for guidance in my life's situation. Strength poured in – the fairies that I had once believed in – returned! It was in actual fact my return – a return to innocence.

87

Ever since my experience of seeing Marta, the old grandmother I had seen while meditating in Secunda, I had a sense of someone looking after me. Whoever she was - it didn't matter, all I knew was that she had become a mother figure to me. I felt as though I could talk to her and she would hear me, sleep and she would be standing by my bed side gently stroking my hair. I felt safe.

Different experiences started happening after I decided to surrender to the fact that time didn't really exist. I started experiencing *past lives* and they become more and more frequent. It freaked me out and I was convinced I was either going mad or that the demons were taking over my mind! How could this be possible, I had never been taught about all this *stuff* before? I had told David about my visions of Martha and to him it was a normal phenomenon.

It was about a month after seeing her for the first time that David and I walked into a large bookstore where thousands of books were on display. I was angry – angry with life – angry with all these visions that I was having – angry with all this *bull shit* of past life experiences! I had come to point in my life that I had experienced enough and determined that I would never every allow myself to be 'opened' to these demonic enteritis ever again.
Without analytically observing which isle or category, Author or title I was storming toward, I opened the first book I could find. There I glared upon a very familiar face - a face I had found comfort in - the face of Marta.
I felt as though I was about to faint as I read the description below her picture which described who she was – *"A North American woman named Martha holding a medicine pipe that she passed on to her daughter."*
From that day on I never questioned or doubted the images and information that I was given. I had always prayed to find my calling

and now I knew. I knew that the path that I was about to walk would be a lonely one - One that never had many followers, but a path that I had been called to walk long before my return to this new body.

LESSONS

Life is a continuous struggle between reality and illusion,
death and life,
faith verses agnostics,
madness fighting sanity.

What is sanity?
Is it a forfeit of an illusion state of being,
or a reality of 'otherness'?

Does one declare denouncement of oneself,
In order to be accepted into a mortuary of freedom,
or credible to be a part of the universal bank of karmic freedom?

Who dictates the truth?

Who is worthy to be the judge of universal energies,
that flutter systematically in non-existence.
yet existed before time and space?

Parallel co-creators,
metaphors of life,
yearning for the same cell,
yet determine the conclusion to be flawed.

ACT TWENTY ONE

--- *Marrying your Soul Mate* ---

From the time that David and I had been together I had told him never to ask me to marry him. I was afraid that what we had would land up in another disaster. I didn't want Cinderbella to go through another divorce, she was living a life of love and happiness after her first divorce why the hell would she want to do it all over again? David made me happy; we laughed and *played* a lot. We were different from the morbid couples who looked 'very married'. Our lives were being healed by being together and teaching each other how it should have been and how love still existed. Both of us were realising that we were worth something, that we could feel alive again. The moments of being together were precious, unconditional and whole.

We had both undergone similar experiences and by now knew without a doubt that we had loved each other for many lives – it was as though we were two souls that had lost each other for a couple of years and then re-united. We might not be the wealthiest of couples but for this moment and time we were in love.

And then it happened – he proposed! At first I was shocked - shocked that he had the audacity to think that he could go and 'stuff it all up'! Sitting at a restaurant I open up this beautifully wrapped small box, a box that visually represented in an exceptional world to be the box that was labelled a 'ring holder'. You know the familiar one that makes your brain scream "run, maiden hide!"

I glared at him and he smiled saying "If it fits you will you marry me?"

I am too dumbfounded to reply.

As I carefully unwrap the box I thought of a million places I would like to hide at this present moment.

And there it is – not a ring but a minute glass slipper that he has had the glass blower design.

On the 8th of August, 1998, we say our new vows to each other and start life *all over again*.

INSEPRABILITY

Is it separation of body that questions our love?
Is it distance that strengthens our dreams?
Is it society's rights and wrongs that keep us a part,
or only our fear that mistakes are all the same?

When you're gone the distance is years
My dreams become realities
Night times are daytimes,
And I experience our dream.
Memories of the past melt away the pain.

In visions I call your name,
stroke your skin,
embrace your body,
smell your warmth,
see your love.
We melt primordially into the future,
shifting time and space,
A preview of things to become.

Proliferate our love
in this prologue called 'life'

Fornication not forfeited,
desires not denounced
Forbidden fruits, sexuality and lust.
engulf this sea of love

Only dreams expose the above nevertheless soon
destiny's conception will propagate our souls.

ACT TWETY TWO

--- *Knowing What You Want* ---

Driving down the panhandle to a house that we have received a repossession listing of, I can feel that this will be our new home. The house is not visible and the only concern that David has at this moment is that it is way above the price that we can afford.

I don't hear a word he is trying to tell me, all I know is that I can *feel* that this *is* our new home.

As we walk around this derelict 750 square meters of building, I am already picturing where I will be hanging each painting. Obviously I take out my tarot cards and ask for guidance.

Affirmation is *shown*.

David being the logical one out of us knows that no matter how many cards, rocks or bones I throw at it this moment in time, it will not be able to give him some magical solution to how he will pay for this home. I am adamant and firmly believing that *if you know what you want you can have it*.

After putting in an offer at the same price that we had both agreed upon, the bank accepts our offer. We have a new home, our very own beautiful 750 square meters of home. After only two weeks of coming across this home, we move in and make it *our home*. I sniggered to myself wondering if this was maybe the gutters that my mother had said I would land up in!

In the past eleven years I have learnt to focus upon my intentions and projections in a way that can '*move a mountain*', timelessly experienced how if you know what you want you **can** have it.

93

Many of us want success but are not willing to work *hard* in order to obtain that success. We firstly have to be passionate about what we are doing in order to make it become successful. Personally I am passionate about writing books and have often spent eighteen hours a day writing the educational books that had to be submitted urgently. Writing twenty four books in five months all on your own is no joke, but having the passion and correct intensions to write those books was what kept me motivated *and determined to do it.*

The new home we lived in had a garage that was 180 square meters. It was a dream comes true, a place where I could start my long wished for art classes.
Continuously I was shown that if there are things that I would love to do in life but at a present moment could not foreseeing the possibilities of them ever being achievable, I would write them down.

Now here's another experiment for you to play around with.
Make a list of these things that you would love to have in life. Don't worry about how they will be accomplished or given – just write down what you want.

In 1997 in my *down and out year*, I wrote a list of four desires that I had.

1. *To start my own art classes*
2. *To teach creative visualisation techniques*
3. *To help people find ways to get in touch with themselves*
4. *To further my studies in art.*

I had no idea of how any of the above would be possible, but I wrote them down, believed that the universe would give me what was correct for me personally in its own time. I didn't try and play God – just wrote them down and left them to unfold in their own time.

In 1998 David enrolled me into UNISA, the University of South Africa, where I spent six years study for a BVA (*Bachelor of Visual Arts*).
By the middle of 1999 I started teaching art and meditation.
In 2000 – 2004 I was actively involved with workshops and seminars, teaching from ICU staff to business persons new ways on how to handle their stress loads.
Each one of my four desires had become a reality –and therefore my motto of what I stood for *if you know what you want you can have it* – proved itself!

INTELLECTUAL PEOPLE

Caged suckers
anticipate their unanswered thoughts,
slice their existence to find more.
More is a fraction of an explosive mind,
Mind is a particle of all
So who knows why,
and is why the all?
Is not life about existing in the now?

ACT TWENTY-THREE

--- *In the End - Nothing Really Matters* ---

The lyrics in songs have always been important to me – I suppose I can put it down to be because my personality lends itself to being one that is analytical yet sensitive traits.

A track from Metallica's Vertigo album is titled *Nothing Else Matters*. This particular song has always had an impact on me, and the words are as follows:-

So close no matter how far
Couldn't be much more from the heart
Forever trusting who we are
And nothing else matters

Never opened myself this way
All these words I don't just say
And nothing else matters

Trust I seek and I find you
Every day something new
Open mind for a different view
And nothing else matters

Never cared for what they do
Never cared for what they know
But I know

How we all yearn to be loved, unconditionally and accepted. Will we ever find this kind of love in another human being? We all pretend to believe in it, but can we really label it as being real? Musicians and artists have written songs of how they will love each other forever, no matter what. Words play an enormous part in our emotional well-being. We all want to belong, love, live - forever - but who knows what the future holds. Once again it all boils down to the same old story. We need to start becoming an *unconditional lover* to the first step to making the difference - *ourselves*.

Mistakes are beautiful, they help us grow and learn. What are mistakes – is there a wrong or a right? Being true to ourselves and loving who we are, unconditionally, will help us realise that all that is important in the end is our own happiness. When we are lying on our death bed, those last few precious moments of our life, what will we remember? Will we really care about all the mistakes that we have made, all the divorces we may have gone through or the marriages that we are in? Will we want to waste our last few minutes stressing over all the things that we would quickly like to rectify or perfect – or will we lie there and ponder over the memories that we spent in love and happiness, or moments that we wished we could re-live; and then smile.

Society pressurises us into believing we must conform. Media has created stereotypes. The ways in which woman used to be in touch with our mother earth have been forgotten and replaced by a *quick fix*. We no longer make time to gaze into a fire and reset our minds or watch the full moon. These are the natural beauties of life. The natural elements that we have been freely given to rebalance us and yet are not even accounted for any more. Why? Where did we go wrong?

In my creative visualisation classes I taught many men and women how to *relearn* what they had forgotten.

As children we instinctively love to play with mud or build sandcastles - this was our instinctive way of *knowing* how the element of earth was beneficial to our well-being.

Running in the wind (air), cooking marshmallows in a fire (fire), swimming in a lake (water) – are among the essential elements that we naturally worked with, played with and enjoyed.
It's never too late to regain and reclaim our strengths and thereby take on a firm stand towards finding our true selves once more.

BURNING FOR LOVE

Dance with me in this flame
Where warmth and death are one
United essences of life brought forth
through surrender

Eternal immortal momentary lights
Swindling ruthlessly, forever.
Elementary pleasures combust as ignited love
Breathing the energetic night
Creating nothingness into ALL

Without you I have no flame,
Cannot dance,
Cease to burn
Wither into discarded ashes
which will lie on our earth and rot

Never forget that through life and death
You are my soul
You are my ALL
Only for one second come dance with me in this flame?
Remember
Remember without mind
Don't judge our discrepancies
Forget the grudges
Throw out the bin
Be with this moment
And come dance with me in the flame.

ACT TWENTY FOUR

Loneliness

Spending an evening having dinner with our two closest friends, Victor and Margie, David and I ask them whether or not they would ever remarry. Neither of the two were connected to each other in any way except for being good friends.

Margie is a fifty six year single mother. Having had her third child, Jessica at the age of thirty eight she still has the responsibilities of fetching and carting, feeding and clothing etc. Many single women her age have their homes to themselves by this age. Margie has been divorced for over twelve years. Through these years she has met numerous men, watched them fall in and out of love with her, dine and wined her, but never found that prince charming that sweeps her off her feet. "It gets lonely on your own," she says "even though I have the company of Jessica, I still yearn for that adult hug, that special touch; you know that sense of *feeling alive!*"

I need my space and know that it's important for me to take time out to do the things I love. As I sit listening to Margie I realise how I so often take David's love for granted. He is the one that I have to hold me, hug me and make me feel alive and yet I acknowledge that I spend times contemplating how wonderful it must be to be a single woman. At night when he snores I think about how wonderful it must be to be alone, a whole massive bed to myself where I can be undisturbed. I've been blessed with a man that gives me the freedom to be me. He has always supported me in my crazy moments.

I love excitement and spontaneous events. It must be hard living with a person like me, even though I don't think so. Some days I get a bee in my bonnet and decide that I would love to fly to Ireland. I live the moment. I phone the agency, search the internet, phone friends and ask them whether they want to join me, visualise myself boarding the aeroplane, touring the countryside, I live the whole experience out. I've never got to fly to Ireland, well not yet, but I've lived it and that's what feels good.

Victor is a fifty five year old, divorced and still living on the same farm as his ex-wife. His marriage life story sounded bizarre when we first heard it. Annette and him had four children and were married for almost fifteen years before they decided to get divorced. A third party; a woman; had fallen in love with Victor while they were still married. Annette was not threatened by having another woman in their lives and they lived under the same roof, together for many months. The two women enjoyed each other's company and shared the same interest, in particular the same man. Now this in today's Western society sounds like a rather awkward situation to be in, but it worked for them. The reason for their getting divorced was not due to the third party but rather an acceptance that they could be better friends being unmarried. They still live on the same property but have given each other the freedom to exploit their own paths. There is no jealousy, anger or resentment between them, even after going through a divorce. Victor has many acquaintances and because of his personality is well-liked.
Victor smiles as he answers our proposed question "The minute we get married something spontaneous disappears. It's important to me not to try and understand the meaning of life and rather experience the exhilaration of being alive."

Different strokes for different folks but like it or not both Margie and Victor need to be loved, it's in our human nature.

The law of attraction plays a huge part in each one's life. Whether or not you are conscious of it or not, if you stop for a moment and analyse your life – past and present – you will see the thin line that connects all events in your life. If we are positive about our lives we attract goings on that have a positive reaction, and vice versa. *What we sow we will reap*. Taking into account the recurring events that have happened since the universe guided me into writing this book, I have noticed that I am drawn toward more and more people that are either getting married, getting divorced or have been divorced. It might be that I am just more conscious of the subject matter but either way I have found it fascinating to be able to hear the different stories.

Sandy a waitress, who I met last night, was glowing as she told me her story. She had met her husband to be over three years ago whilst at university. It was a Valentine's Day dance. He was an exchange student from the United States. They fell in love from the moment of meeting. She is due to be wed in a few months' time and relocate to the States. They haven't seen each other for a whole year, but still have the surety that they love each other. Long distance relationships – there has been so much said.

I met Harry on a bus about three years ago. We had both been up in Johannesburg to visit a spiritual master. Sitting next to him for those five hours while we travelled, I listened to his painful story of how he was about to get divorced. He and his wife Lisa had been married for over ten years. He was totally broken when he learnt how his wife had had an affair with one of his best friends. He blamed himself. He could not come to terms with the fact that this would ever happen to him. Ever since that day we have remained in contact and shared the angers, pains and regrets that he was working through.

Paul, a childhood friend, had three children with his ex-wife. Everything was going right for them. She was a lawyer and he a very successful business man. They lived in the most elite looking home, drove fancy cars and socialised with the Jones's. Coming from a staunch religious background he believed he would be as committed to his marriage as his parents were. Paul believed that nothing would ever come between them as there was nothing that either party needed that they didn't already have. But it did. After fifteen years of marriage his wife files for a divorce. It devastated him. Why had it gone wrong? He had given her all the freedom that she needed, was not possessive, caring, supportive, financially secure, hardworking, good looking, sensitive and loving. Loving – then how could she leave him for someone new that she claimed to love – love more than him! It's been over two years since there divorce came through and he still hasn't got over the issue. Why – because he can't believe it happened to him!

I received a message from a friend while driving to Tzaneen to attend a meeting:

Never take some one for granted.
Hold every person close to your heart
because you might wake up one day
and realise that you've just lost a diamond
while you were too busy collecting stones

Sitting in my hotel room I think of how so many men and women, in their different relationships are all searching for the same thing – love! Each one, in their own way wants to feel important, to feel alive and be loved. Many marriages become stale after only a few years. The responsibilities of life - be they children, finances, working conditions etc., can have a huge impact.

The once kind, loving prince returns home from work, exhausted after a long day's work only to find that his princess has become a nag. The kids feel like monsters, the castle has lost its spark. He wants out of there, needs to get to the pub or phone that sexy secretary that smiles at him no matter what! Then on the other hand the once upon a time princess doesn't get the attention that she so longs for, He never tells her she looks beautiful, he's too busy watching the sports channel, he comes home after work and expects his dinner even if she too has had a hard long day. They go to bed with miserable faces, and sometimes even in different rooms. They wake up in the morning and yearn for that extra five minutes that they can cover their heads under their pillows and believe that they are actually dead!

The wife's been begging him to listen to her about something that she feels is important. He on the other hand is too tired to hear the same non-logical emotional dilemma that she feels that she has. He can't understand how a woman can be so empathic about a situation or emotion and puts it down to the fact that she's either experiencing PMT or going through menopause. Feeling rejected she escapes into her silence and vows that in order to prevent a confrontation again, she'll just let it be. While walking down the supermarket isle she notices a gorgeous man smiling at her or bumps into Jonnie that she hasn't seen for years. They have coffee together and talk. Yes they talk! This is the most amazing time of her life, the feeling of being able to say just how you feel and the very fact that someone out there is willing to listen. How easy it is to have an affair. Especially when you've reached the point that you don't even care anymore. You've given up trying to work on that marriage that died the day you put the slipper on. Having that affair makes you feel alive again, a

princess a 'real person, one that you thought you would be forever –
but the consequences that follow could well leave you in a worse
situation than you ever imagined possible.

The kids are sliced into particles that are dependent on the court's
decision. The house, the cars, the whole lot comes crumbling down –
why – all because he wouldn't listen? There's no guarantee to a
marriage lasting forever but what does count is that if there's a will
there's a way. Starting off by making the decision that you want it to
work, that you want to give it what it takes to make a happy and long
lasting marriage is the starting point to that new day. Putting the past
behind and deciding to put into it what you would expect to have, not
get back, takes a lot of guts. Our minds are the greatest computers,
we can store every bit of information we choose. We can hold onto
the fears, the regrets, the negative situations of who said what and
who was wrong, or alternatively we can push the button that says
delete. Having an affair with the person you are married to can
become quite a challenge and adventurous to both parties. Imagine
that this man, the one that you said "I love you until the day we die",
just happens to be the diamond that you have.
Start nurturing it with new eyes and make it feel as though it is the
greatest gift you've ever received and will ever receive. Don't look
at the flaws but rather at the beauty that can be yours forever. You
have to change the impression in your mind, not the diamond. It's
your choice!

YEARNING FOR APPRAISAL

Estimate your fucked up state, then multiply it by nine..

Demise the equation of sanity then divide it by ten.

Who is the joker,

Who is the judge?

What are you aching for?

Who decides the verdict?

Why so many formulas

Contradicting the truth

Substituting reality

Momentarily in time.

Tuning into that emptiness

Equating the conclusion

Valuating segments of

Fragmented illusions.

Sustaining hope

Beating conditionally

Who holds the ruling?

You should know!

ACT TWENTY FIVE

------- *Undoing the Past*-------

Growing up most girls play with *Barbie* dolls- I could not wait to get home from school and run next door where my friends and I spent endless hours living in our *Cinderbella* worlds. Our *Barbie's* would get engaged to the *Kens*, and experience the excitement of being whisked off in their fancy sports cars and living happily ever after. These Barbie's and Kens were real, they were alive and they helped us to create visual images of how when we grow up one day, our lives would also be.

No wonder when Charles proposed I had no fears! I signed the necessary contracts without even considering whether or not I was being screwed-over– only to find out six years down the line that in actual fact I was - only after threatening to leave him, was it changed. That's life. And what do all the past hurts do to us – make us become more afraid of getting hurt again! Second, third, fourth or a million time around it will still be the same – what we need to do is get to the point where we stop blaming our past for our present fears. Taking those fears into the next relationship isn't going to make it any better for us or the new one that we promise "*'til death do us part"*.

We need to analyse our own hurts and come to terms with our lessons that we have received from them, thereby creating a healing to any situation rather than one of fear, *hurts, mistrust, angers,* and so the list goes on. We need to question ourselves and ask what it is that we are really fearing – where does it stem from- and why?

I always had a fear of *rejection*. It took me a long time making peace with my fear. While teaching creative visualisation and art therapy classes I spent many hours in either *self*-introspection or meditation.

Teaching others allowed me to teach myself, remind myself and thus - heal myself. I started finding out more about my childhood, digging deep into the past to find the foundation of my present fears. Finding out about how my mother was suicidal and at one stage so close to blowing her brains out, made me understand how emotions stem as far back as being an embryo. Sensing my mother's pains, feelings and hurts while still connected to her umbilical cord were one of the many incidences that I had to make peace with. I had to overcome my own fears of the rejection I might have had to experience. Now no one is perfect and I'm not trying to insinuate that my own mother might have been responsible for my insecurities, but what I will say is that we have to let go – let go of trying to blame. We have to come to terms with *who we really are, have always been* and *will be* in the future – if we can just let go. We are not a soul in a body, we are the All. If we are the All then what are we fearing? We have the right to be happy, fearless and free. *You are responsible for your own happiness through the choices and decisions that you make as long as you have a **reason and purpose behind them**!*

Making the decision to let go of your parts by dealing with your fears, angers, hurts and emotions is the first step to rediscovering *self.* Many of the students that I taught went through the deep searching stage, and opened up emotions that they didn't even think were part of what they called 'personality traits'. Some experienced angers that were so suppressed before. They allowed themselves to cry, to laugh to be angry or whatever they felt. They learnt that they didn't have to care about what people thought – they were allowed to be happy – to be childlike again. Anton was a reserved student in his mid-forties, I presume. He never spoke to any of the other students. No one ever got to know him, he never allowed any one into his life. By the way he dressed I assumed that he must be a business man The art therapy classes began at six and he would always be punctual, dressed in his suit and white shirt. It bothered me in the beginning, as I was afraid that he might get them all messed up, but said nothing. I was the teacher and not the mother and so often had to remind myself of that. Working with his self-portrait he silently drew out his emotions. They were dark and morbid, but I was starting to get to know him – without words.

Glen on the other hand was a vibrant computer guy. He was Chinese and had a specialness about him. His work was colourful and after about the third week of working with his self-portrait he approached me after class. He complained about the fact that ever since he had started dealing with himself by painting his self-portrait, he found that he had become tearful. It worried him as he was not that type of person. *Big boys don't cry*.

I assured him that he needs to be with whatever emotions he experienced. Not to analyse them just yet but simply let them take their natural course. As we start dealing with emotions I realise that this extrovert impression we all had assumed he was, is actually the total opposite. He admits to his fears and confesses that he has a fear of *self-worthlessness*.   He had been experiencing tremendous frustration at work. His biggest dream was to be in a situation that he could use his skills but feared that he wasn't good enough.   Six months down the line he is offered the most incredible opportunity in his field - grown to accept his *self-worth* and no longer has the insecurities that he once believed he would never overcome.

I was grateful to the universe to allow me to be a channel and witness so many men and women heal themselves. We all have pasts but when we experience how beautiful it feels once we've let go of the things in our lives that have weighed us down, we will wonder why we had held on to them for so long.

SNAKE

Twisted fortune
terrifies memories
unleashing venom
of treacherous fangs
that latch to fearful flaws.

Hypocritical sensations
slither momentarily
Monotonous motherhood
Umbilical connection
That attaches bond to blood.

Your venom
Saturates my veins
And still I conquer not.

Hissing whips
Strap my body not
Unleashed torture
Mesmerised in an un-hypnotised consciousness.

ACT TWENTY SIX

--------For the Love of it-------

Since a child I was passionate about art. Deep down inside me I believed that one day I would become a famous illustrator and show the world life through visual images.

After my divorce I had contacted *Maskew Miller Longman and Heinemann* Publishers in England. I sent through some of my illustrations and they loved them. Even though I have mentioned that I had the fear of rejection, I realised it wasn't the only one. I froze and that was the last time they heard from me. David kept begging me to just do it, but I was too afraid - afraid of success. I had to learn to *undo* what I had been taught. I wasn't the one that was supposed to be the bread winner; I wasn't the one that was supposed to be talked about – I was a woman.

My mother had never worked – she was happy to play the role of being mother and wife. I had followed in her footsteps – until I left Charles! I was scared as this was all so new to me – I wondered if I had done the right thing – maybe I should have stayed in a protected normal situation – one that was familiar – one that kept me feeling safe!

But the universe knew best. I received a phone call a few years later. Meeting Dr Hasan, a doctor in Linguistics, at a real dilapidated restaurant, I show him my portfolio. He tells me about a *'Tender'* that government has released requesting for Black Publishing Companies to write educational books. He is looking for an illustrator and because the company is newly established cannot pay me but gives me his word that if our 'Tender' be accepted, we will be greatly rewarded. As he looked me in the eyes he said "Just trust me".

Looking at the situation from an analytical point of few and seeing that this man who claims to be a doctor, has no car, is down and out and cannot pay me – you would probably be thinking exactly what David did when I return home and told him that I had accepted and was committing myself to work hard for something that I had a passion for – children and learners in South Africa. 'Babe, you are crazy, how can you trust a man you don't even know?' I smiled and he knew then that I wasn't going to let anyone stop me. Sometimes we get an inside voice that says "you go for it!" - And I did!

The day we got informed that our 'Tender' had been accepted was as exciting as the part from Grimm's Fairy tales where *Cinderella* tries on the slipper and it fits! Our '*slipper*' fitted so perfectly – and an opportunity to dress up in fine gowns was waiting right in front of us.

Establishing and building our publishing company has been something that has been fulfilling and challenging for both Dr Hasan and myself. Three years after submitting our first set of Educational Books, I receive a phone call from his wife. They have had to amputate his leg. Having worked so hard and being under so much pressures Dr Hasan developed gangrene due to him being a diabetic. My heart aches as I listen to the news.

There are many sacrifices that life challenges you with; especially if you don't keep a balance. Male or female that isn't the issue – the issue lies with whether or not you know when to tighten or loosen the reins. There's a very fine line between the two.

So many people wish for success yet so few are willing to work hard to get it. Pacing yourself is the name of the game. Working hard to get it – this does not mean that the harder you work, the more you worry, the more you stress or have sleepless nights about a situation or task that you have to complete – it simply means being in tune with the belief that it will come to you in its own time. I have been a firm believer in "*If you know what you want you can have it*".

Through time I have learnt that by worrying about a particular situation, for instance getting my educational books out on time because of the deadlines, didn't make it any better. I knew what the deadlines were and therefore in order to ensure that the books were at the printers by the due date, I would have to pace myself and set timeframes accordingly. Stressing about the situation would only add to the anxieties and therefore produce a less creative flow into my work.

Having the personality that I do, I often find myself worrying about everything as though it's a huge *big bubble* that is bound to burst sooner or later - and then the bubble pops and I'm left with nothing. Due to this I've had to train myself to pace myself and change my mind-set into a structural positive process whereby I can allow myself the sense of a logical 'safety zone' to become the beginning of that which I wish to achieve. Often I would find that it got so bad that I would catch myself in a mind-set that I would worry about the fact that I didn't have anything to worry about! It was almost as if I didn't have anything to stress about, and therefore worry because I felt that there must be something wrong.

I presumed that the energy and effort that I was putting into stressing about something would determine my success or failure in any given situation. After hitting my head against many walls I began to realise that the answer lay in learning to let go - to accept that if my thoughts were positive I would attract positive situations. I started believing that the universe would take care of me and that by doing my part in a loving and rightful mind-set I would be rewarded accordingly.

So many times I have tried to play *God*. I wake up early to ensure that I have enough time to get dressed, relax myself before the scheduled appointment with a friend. Make sure that everything is in order so that I can have time out, drive down the mountain to the restaurant we will be meeting at, sit down at least a half an hour before she arrives and then – oh yes then, she cancels saying she's had other things come up out of her control! Do I get angry and tell her this will be the last date we ever pre arrange – or do I breathe? I breathe- this is the way I am trying to come to grips with the why's. It's always taken time for me to react and in most cases I generally have to process things before reacting. Whether this is a good or bad thing, I try and think of it as neither, and accept that it is just the way I personally deal with life. Generally, I sit and contemplate and try and 'get in touch with my inner grammar'. Yes, I'm annoyed; irritated that she/he has wasted my time, think of all the other things that I could have done, should have done, and then surrender. Surrender to the fact that I cannot always control every single situation. I stop trying to play God and know that the universe knows best.

My mother always had a saying that insinuated that "*everything happens for a reason*" and her other one was "*When one door closes, the other one opens*".
Sooner or later we have to learn how to surrender to the circumstances that we cannot control and leave it up to the universal

mystery who knows all. There are reasons for everything and every situation even if we don't always find out the answers. By just accepting the *now* for being the only important time for the rest of our lives, we begin to get in touch with that peace that we so often lose out on because we are either stressing about something that hasn't even happened, may never happen and really isn't important - now.

Just having the desire for life, to appreciate the now - the only present time that exists, will allow you the choice of what you want to hold on to or what you want to release.

Having cancer was a choice. I allowed myself to become ill, but I also chose to live. Choosing life gave me a reason to live one day at a time, blaming x, y or z would not have made matters any better, but the decision that from this day onwards I will live a *happy and appreciate my precious life*, gave me new hope and set me free from the cancer that was eating me up.

There are many illnesses, and I am not qualified in the fields of medicine to make a statement or even conceptualise the causes or symptoms of even a few of them, but what I do know is that the way I handled mine made the difference, logically, medically and spiritually.

Changing the symptoms by changing my attitude gave me new life, new dreams and a hope to live my life to its full potential. I had a desire and through this desire I made the changes. It was my attitude that made the difference.

Through the years while working in Johannesburg and visiting patients in hospital I was able to share my story with them. My story was not their story and could never be. They had the choice to listen and use what they needed to hear, or alternatively, to reject and not use.

No one person can give you your answers. Your story is your own story but when we understand the *all or the whole* is interconnected we will be able to see our lives as part of the bigger picture. Let me give you an example – let's say that you live in this country village where once there was only a handful of people. The sewage system is maintained by ensuring that each person maintains their own septic tank. The village can only hold a specific number of people at a given time otherwise ...... well sure you can out the picture together for yourself. A few years down the line the balance is out, and I mean totally out! It has become a village that attracts tourists and therefore the once quaint little village that can only occupy a certain limit of residents transforms into a money making business. Hotels have been built, homes have become priceless, more and more people occupy the same space. The ground hasn't grown; the sewage system hasn't changed but who cares! What will eventually happen, yes you get the picture, all 'shit' will break out and the land that once was priceless will become unusable and worthless. The water from the boreholes will become toxic and eventually they might even have to declare the town a disaster area.

The same goes for our bodies. We have to ensure that we take care of its maintenance. We often hear our soft internal voice saying slow down, get rid of the 'shit', what are you holding on to, etc. etc., but we neglect it telling ourselves that only the tough survive and in order to be part of the clan we must push through. So we ignore the warning signs, we suppress the emotional self-inflicted sabotages and carry on. Carry on until what? Eventually the *'shit' hits the fan* and if you lucky it might just not be too late. Life is hard, yes we all know that, and when finances get tight or the interest rates get higher we feel that we need to do one thing to compensate them – work harder!

Living with a cynical partner makes it somewhat more difficult. There have been times in the near past when I could *feel* that things were getting to the point that they were ready to explode. Being the *emotional dreamer*, if that's what society wants to classify me as, I felt that maybe I was being over sensitive.

Not knowing which direction to turn to I found myself becoming more and more isolated from the actual *cause*. We were just not getting on. The more we tried to speak about the situation the worse it became.

My mother had taught us as children never to go to bed having grudges or angers against another. This is easier said than done. Many a night I resorted to sleeping on the futon in my meditation room. This became my *sacred space*, my space where I could be with my own hurts and fears - a space free from all confrontation. I lay thinking and worrying about our relationship. Sometimes woman probably worry more than a man, or maybe they just worry in a different way. In my conclusions that I made while lying awake late at night I believed that men and woman just spoke different languages.

I wondered if I would ever meet a man that could truly understand me and I him. It became an emotional altercation – in this case I confronted my own emotions, analysing them intensely. Where did you go wrong this time Deanne, how come you keep attracting relationships that last for a couple of years and then they all land up the same way? I questioned my love for the man I was with, the man that I had spent over eleven years with – were they a waste of time – had I sold my soul again – maybe I should have rather just have had an affair because by being faithful to a partner just wasn't working out and in the long run the confrontations are all the same any way – why had I got re-married when I knew that marriage wasn't for me –

118

why this why that! The mental list went on for ever. I made up my mind that I loved him and therefore the sacrifices that I had to make were worth it. We would give it a month of complete dedicated quality commitment and then decide where and what route to take. This was the strangest part of our relationship – we both claimed to have one thing in common – *that we loved each other*!

It confused me – how could two people have such conflicting thoughts and behaviour and yet still claim to love each other?

I have always had the personality of being the teacher, the nurturer, the counsellor to my friends and students and yet here I was not even able to help myself! Where had I gone wrong? How did I allow this to eventually get so far? I, me! *Blame, guilt, and anger* – these were the emotions and accusations that filled my scene. The show had gone bad, the audience had left and I sat in a whirlwind of confusion and *loneliness* once more.

I call up my friend Ann, asking her to come away with me for a few days.

And so we leave for the game reserve the following day. She has been such a comforter in my life. I don't trust very easily and when meeting someone for the first time I tend to lean to the sceptical side first before throwing myself into becoming a new acquaintance. It's not that I don't enjoy meeting new people it's just that letting them into my *space* takes a bit more time than normal.

Excited to be away in the bush
Dancing
Same language
Scheming
Nothing changes

Book into Boondocks
Walk labyrinth
New moon
Write 13 page letter
Come up with new ideas
Knowing what you want and putting it out into the universe
Art gallery
Send off emails
Go to Johannesburg
Start morning pages
Living a fulfilled live by changing your focus

SHE IS

In inner silence I salute the heroin
as she relinquishes attachments
and gracefully slithers as she wavers her skin
to become who she always was
and now is

Flying freely - no returning back to her
Caterpillar-like state of the past
Instead her virgin wings glitter in the sunlight
heart pulsates the beat of earths call

Baptised by the morning dew
She breathes her first breath of newness
No regrets as the cocoon sets her loose.
No afterbirth
No past
Her new colours reward her victory

She is
And always was

ACT TWENTY SEVEN

-------Full Circle-------

Life is full of unexpected events. The strangest thing about unexpected events is that when we analyse them they aren't as unexpected as we make them out to be. Over a year ago I remember telling David that there were going to be changes regarding working with our Productions Company. I could not quite 'put my finger on' why I felt that way. Things were going well and our company was growing but my *gut* feelings warned me to prepare for change.

It was the busiest year in our publishing company that I could ever recall, and after writing over twenty-four educational books in less than five months, I was exhausted. The little soft voice inside my head kept on repeating itself "prepare for change" but analytically I could not work it out.

Our end of year, Company meeting, gave me new hope. My partner and I discussed the growth of the business and how we would be creating new sub-branches into all the provinces throughout South Africa. I was excited about *taking on* the Mpumalanga Province, as this is the place we live. It would mean recruiting new authors and becoming totally engulfed with the new venture. This was my dream and seeing it happening in a span of less than six years felt so rewarding. To me it wasn't about the money, it was about seeing the rewards of our commitment and trust. The same man that had walked into my life and told me to trust him was now still standing beside me and we were growing – together.

In Africa we have a saying about time which means that things happen according to the place we live in – we call it "African time" - well this is what you get used to and learn to not try and change the cultural ways. Early this year my partner and I draw up a contract at the lawyers. We are told that it would take approximately three to four weeks for everything to be 'signed and sealed'. Some seven months down the line and still - no signed contract. Now this may be hard to imagine, especially if you don't live in Africa, but Africa or not the universe knows best.

The lawyer's offices had been broken into and all contracts and documents needed to be re-drawn. If you have ever worked in a publishing company you will know the various procedures that we go through, and therefore time is something you can never have enough of. In our case with a partner that lives almost seven hundred kilometres away in a remote area, you can imagine that it is not always as easy as getting into a car and making an appointment with a lawyer to re-structure a contract. The day eventually arrives and sitting in the lawyer's office is like experiencing a dejavu - the only difference is that this time I am uneasy. I cannot understand why - there is no logical reason - it just is. Changes are made on the contract – again we will have to wait.

David warns me that there is a bigger picture to this whole situation, I reassure him that everything will be just fine, even though my gut feel agrees that things are not right. Being a woman that works in a reasonably big business enterprise, I tend project a sense of I am 'capable, independent and have everything under control'. So having a husband that tries to 'tell' me that things are not under *control* often tends to push my wrong buttons. I need to find out things for myself – in my own way- in my own time – and not be told by anyone else. It could even just be a personality trait, who cares, but that's just the way I am. You know that horrible word that you don't want to acknowledge called 'ego'! Shortly after the meeting I phone my dear friend Ann. She being a book keeper and a logical woman I feel would understand best. And so we begin discussing the contract and she reassures me that there is nothing to worry about and that the new venture will be successful - logically. Methodically I start 'putting my house in order', phone the printers, and contact the relevant persons in Government to inform them that I will be directing the new branch of our Production Company.

Less than a week later I find myself sitting back in the same lawyer's office – this time with a different case. After over six years of loyalty and trust I 'D.K.F' have been betrayed – betrayed by yet another person that I believed I could trust – my very own business partner

Sourcing information to set up the Mpumalanga branch I learn that not only have most of my written books been plagiarised and sold under my partner's son's name, but that millions of Rands have been made without my knowing. Now I don't want to bore you with my emotions but if you have gone through a divorce you would probably understand the pains. It's the same *stuff* – the very stuff that women are made of – the stuff that gets taken away when you are betrayed. Betrayal leaves you feeling like you've just been raped - as though your very life's purpose has been stolen away. It creates visuals of blackness that want to be buried so deep down, yet still continuously keep resurfacing in the forms of different emotions. The blame that you put yourself through, the guilt that comes like an aftermath of an explosion or earthquake. Who do you turn to that can fully understand even for just one second what you are really experiencing? - no one. You are the only one that can physically, spiritually and emotionally experience the feelings. You may have friends and family that can comfort you during these times but they can never truly have the actual experience of how you personally feel inside.

In the past whenever I have experience some type of emotional hurt, I have learnt that the best way for me to deal with the present circumstance is to withdraw and isolate myself in an environment where I can get clarity. This has meant either going for a walk alone in the mountains for a couple of hours or resorting to retreat. There I would go and pray to the God the great spirit for guidance and wisdom. I would allow myself time to reconnect to the *Self*, my very essence of existence. It gave me the space to find myself, to be able to see the *bigger picture* of any situation that I found myself in, and thereafter return with clarity.

And so as previously mentioned, my mother's favourite quotation of *'everything happens for a reason',* tests me once more. To some it may just be a *saying*, but when you become submissive to the higher powers – the powers that are larger than yourself yet a part of your very existence - you start learning to submit and begin to give thanks, even during times of trail and tribulation. It's not always as easy as it may sound - you don't just go through a betrayal and say "Oh, thank you higher forces for allowing me to go through this betrayal". No, it hurts. You feel and experience the hurts and the mind in the process can become a very powerful tool. It just never wants to stop talking. When you tell yourself you need to switch off from the drama, *mind* stands and snarls at you saying "try me, baby!" It's like a warfare that goes on and on forever – causing battles, bleeding, angers and pains. Until you eventually shout at *it* "I've had enough, get behind me Satan!" Sternly pulling that pillow over your head, you drop off to sleep and experience a peace which feels to you like *Nirvana*.

In the long run when you have gone through the dilemma, you often will be shown the reasons of why a certain event occurred during a specific era. Sometimes you may not, aren't meant to or who knows the billion other explanations that can be explained by philosophisers and logistical analysers – but if you have **faith** that your path is there for you to *walk* and *learn* from - even through times of loneliness - you will experience that you become a stronger person and that the *gifts* that you receive from standing up for your choices are more rewarding than going according to logics. It's about trusting in your*self /in the God of all understanding.* Allowing the presence of the universal energies to guide and protect you in whatever situation that you are in or will be in time to come.

It is amazing how these *gut feelings, intuitive guidance's,* always know what is best for us. Different traditions and religion groups practise various techniques to generate and project a sense of protection. No matter what you want to call them they boil down to the same essence – *prayer and belief.* You could pray for a certain topic and ask for clarity, but if you do not have *faith* it will never manifest. Faith is about believing that no matter what, it **will** manifest. The word I like to use and have used for many years is projection. Projecting that a situation *will* happen - that is for the good of all and to harm none - allows me to have faith that it is not in my hands but up to the higher guiding forces, universal energies, Great Spirit, or call it what you want. I ask for what I need, clarify it, believe and then trust in the forces to continue in their own way. It takes the pressures off me; it's like having a protector twenty-four hours a day. So often we try playing God, and then when we are finally burnt out and run down we remember that this was never our *role* in life. All we are responsible for is to play our part in the play and don't to have to act out everyone else's roles too.

Fire is one of the fundamental earth elements that I have the strongest connection to. Having used it as an instrument to do my biddings I have noticed that it has the energetic powers to remove negative situations as well as draw in positive changes. Fire has been used by many traditions and cultures in the past.

In Africa many years ago, the settlers used to make a fire at night to protect themselves from the wild animals. The North American Indians used it as a divination tool and a connector to Great Spirit. Fire is acknowledged by some to be the element of the South. It is symbolic of the protector - the protector that stands in the South- the fire within- the fire above and below.

Being conscious of our surroundings and the changes that occur in nature can often assist and guide us to *see* clearer. A day before seeing the lawyer with regards to the plagiarism etc., a fire devastatingly burnt many hectares of forest and dwellings in and around our residential village. The wind was not beneficial to the circumstances as it howled at over 90 kilometres an hour. Nearby villages evacuated their homes and resorted to stay in our village until further notice. People huddled together as they prayed for their belongings to be saved from burning. The things that they had hurriedly packed before evacuating were generally the possessions that were most important to them at this stage of their lives. Ann arrived in her car with her four cats and two dogs – all her material possessions at this stage were not considered to be of any value!

Fire allows for transformation – introspection – change. It burns the old to make room for the new. Is it not weird how we make our little personal collections and dwellings seem so tactile and important until we are challenged by nature's elemental forces? Earthquakes, tornados, fires, floods, hurricanes are among the many forces that humans stand little chance against. We can't exactly say to the fire "hey Mister Fire, please do not burn my make-up in my house because it's something that I just recently purchased and it's really important to me".

No, fire is fire and when unable to be kept under control due to natures choice, will run its course until it decides it's duty is done.

And even in this devastating event, a positive phenomenon occurred that could be sensed around the village – they were all together, supporting each other emotionally, physically and spiritually without any sense of ranking.

Looking back now I have realised that not only was the fire a metaphor of change in their lives but an icon of my present betrayal. The fire showed me how it had brought change, transformation and led me to a place of inner introspection. I had to return to my place where I could retreat, the place that I could step aside once again and find the answers to my *true* purpose in life. We are all part of this bigger picture – we just merely have to obtain this balance.

While in India I asked an eastern master a question "Master, when do we know that our *karma* is complete with a certain person? Do we have to come back many lives until this *karma* is complete and relive the whole *karmic* action out until we have made peace with it or do we have a choice to walk away?' He smiled and said "Sister, you definitely have choice. It's like going window shopping – when you have no more *desires* to buy any more items you will no longer need to go window shopping. You will not have to come back when you are finished with those desires and you will have completed full circle. It is only our *attachments* and *desires* that keep us coming back."

I had come full circle with my business partner; and life being a continuous journey, I would soon learn that I had come full circle with David too.

BETRAYAL

I trusted you
I gave you my soul
You trusted me
You gave me your word

I trusted you
I stood by your side
You trusted me
And yet you lied

I trusted you
I never betrayed
You trusted money
Now reap what you have paid.

ACT TWENTY-EIGHT

--- *Finding My Emptiness* ---

Over one and a half years have passed since I last put pen to paper on this book; it was too sore to write positive motivational words when I myself was completely broken and empty.

David and I divorced a few months ago and the normal ups and downs of the 'detaching' went with it. For me it felt like I was the only one in the world who ever had to go through so much pain and hurt, and yet through time I realised it was all part of my life's journey. It's not as easy as it sounds and not that simple when you in the actual situation and even songs like "Everybody Hurts", composed by REM hardly help you to feel any better while you're so low down.

Hurt was not a dramatic enough word to express the depth of the pain that I as well as many others have gone through. To me it felt like the longest death, disaster, dream/nightmare that I could ever describe or put into words.

On top of it all I refused to *accept* it! It could never happen to me – not again! Maybe I could patch it up – cut –cut- cut; rewind, replay, perfect the part and make the ending as all *pretty* stories go – *and they lived happily ever after*- The end- Finale- Finished- Closed book- Closed chapter- Closed door- Closed end, dead end or "oh shit, what now, no not me! "Oh my lord this is real!"

And that's the part I have got to now. The *play* of life becoming a reality- or is it really?

130

After divorcing David my daughter and I remained in our common house. Those months felt like a lifetime and every day I was praying that my prince would return and hold me in his arms. He would kiss me as I lay in my glass coffin and I would awake and ride into the moonlight on the white horse to our castle where we would live in peace   –   forever.   Forever?

Well after spending his 50th birthday with his family in Scotland and returning back to South Africa I convinced him that yes, we had made a huge mistake and that we need to start afresh. Sure I loved him, how does one just stop loving someone that you have spent so many years with?

It was an exciting day and I cleaned my *sacred little space* immaculately. He was returning! I was alive! This must be the happiest day I can remember other than the day the tooth fairy brought me 5c in my pink slipper! Wow incredible this had to go down in all future history books!

How many couples have you heard of that get divorced and then get back together so that they can spend their hopes and dreams of *sitting on that veranda together when they are old and grey!*
We held each other for hours and touched each familiar hair on each other's bodies. He seemed to have gotten greyer but we laughed as we joked about *'oh well, that's what happens when things like this occur'.*

We promised to never allow it to ever happen to us again and that through thick and thin we would make it this time round. We redesigned our living conditions. I would play the scene of the 'girl' that he had once upon a time met many years ago and he would play the mighty warrior, the provider, and the protector.

131

It felt good and I believed that this would help us keep a balance. In the past we had both become so absorbed in our own work situations that we barely had time to greet each other as we passed along the corridor.

My rose garden became my new play den. It was wonderful waking up for the first few weeks and knowing that yes, everything will be just fine. Fine? Is this the dramatic word that expresses emptiness? Apparently so! What was happening? I really, really, really a trillion times over thought that all would work out to be the way it was meant to be. Yes, and that's just it!

So often we decide what our life's plan *should be*! We are stubborn, selfish creatures of habit and we refuse to '*let go and let God have His way*'. We want to control, pre-plan, project our present and future without ever considering whether or not it is in actual fact for the good of *all* and that it harms none or maybe it's just because we are too frightened that our big egos get a little damaged and that we are too afraid to *accept* our *soul's lessons* and *grow*.

Many times we can see the word 'grow' in another context too. It might become that we even need to grow up and face the realities of life! To me this sure has been true! Even the word 'accept' can play a huge part in our life's lessons if we allow it to. I once read a description of how the word should be analysed in our own life. In a précis version it went something like this: -
'*We have two hands that are carrying an item that we cannot let go of. We consider it to be so important even though deep down in our hearts we know that it serves us no purpose. A kind stranger comes along and offers us a new item that is priceless and yet he/she wants to give it to us for free. We cannot receive the gift until we put down*

132

the one we are carrying. We cannot accept the gift until we have allowed ourselves the freedom of putting the other item down. We cannot fully appreciate the gift until we have used our senses to totally absorb each unique part.'

I recall reading in one of the many books that I have read, another illustration of life's journey. To date I cannot recall who the author was or how the actual story went, but I will write it as a new interpretative version: -

*'There once was a woman who cried to the skies 'show me the land of freedom'. Her inner guidance led her to a river bank. As she stood at the edge watching the raging water hit angrily against the river banks, a still voice inside her instructed her to remove all her clothing if she wishes to enter the land of freedom. Without a hesitation she removed her last once of clothing and shouted out "I am ready!" But alas the voice replied "No, look down at your breasts. Only when you are prepared to let go of all will you see the way to the land of freedom!" As she bowed her head and stroked the little man that suckled so serenely from her nipple, tears shed to the earth below and formed a pool of mud. How could she leave him behind – he needed her- she was his comforter and his life-force! This was the choice that she would have to make. The time had come that she had to **allow** herself the right to follow her own destiny. As she pulled him from her nipple his clenching teeth drew blood from her naked body. She refused to allow herself to carry him any longer; she knew it was time for him to grow too. And there before her very eyes, stretched a golden bridge of light that led her to the land of freedom and guided her to fulfil her precious life.*

Accepting and *growing* can lead to many new avenues in our personal life's journey but how much of ourselves we are prepared to surrender to the *All*, the time that it will take us to face our own life's calling and how much of our so called 'comfort zones' and 'ego's' we are prepared to give up in order to find the *'land of freedom'* - depends entirely on each individual. Please don't misunderstand what I am trying to bring across here - I am not insinuating that every woman should step out of their marriage, hit the highway and live with their inner purpose – no – this is not the case. It is only for us to become aware of our own unique qualities and live in that peace completely and in balance where we are in tune with ourselves and the universal changes can therefore become seen as for our best cause not our worst enemies. We need to get to the point that we prioritise our life according to our own circumstances.

Each person will vary and each of us tells a different story, some in a similar manner, but in the end there is one thing that we all share in common, male or female - and that is that we are destined to leave this planet and *go yonder*. This reality should allow us the opportunity to 'take stock of our life' and 'see' where we are not allowing ourselves the opportunity to grow in order to one day become that beautiful light-being that we already are but have forgotten to believe in! Yes, we are souls passing through this life in a human body! That is exciting news and we should wake up each morning knowing that today is the day that no matter where we are, who we are – rich or poor, we all *count* and can make a difference but first we have to start by loving our*selves!*

We are immortal souls and through acknowledging this we can allow ourselves to become *whole-beings* as we fulfil our designated purpose while we walk on mother earth.
It's not *how much we do* to make the difference that counts; it's *what we do* to make the difference that counts. It begins with our attitude towards every given circumstance that may arise. We are faced with choices that can create the shift from negative to positive or vice

versa. There is an old saying that goes *"God never gives us more than we can handle"*. I must admit that I have often thought that God must have seriously have become confused on who he had given x, y and z to! There have been times that I felt that I just could not take any more, but hey I did and I continue each day to almost expect God to hit me with some new challenges just to push me to my limits.

We are not perfect and I don't know of many pure souls that have never ever experienced a bad day. We do get weak; we are designed that way. I believe that even if we were to read every *Self Help*, positive motivational book on every shelf on this earth, we would still have those days that we just wish we could close our eyes and escape from this crazy world of madness. What does matter is that we allow ourselves the challenge of pulling ourselves out of that gloom and doom and putting on our shining armour again and go walk our talk and talk our walk in whatever way we feel will may make that difference to the *All*.

We should strive to become an extension of the light that abides in our fleshly bodies instead of focusing on the scary monsters that hide in the fears of darkness.

Breakfast came and went, lunch, dinner and sleep, in the same old fashion. After spending a few weeks together David and I slowly slipped into the *emptiness* once more. This emptiness was one of the many other factors that had initially determined our final decision to proceed with the divorce.

I am sure that many reading these lines know exactly what this *emptiness* feels like. It's that emptiness which you try and sweep into a corner and pretend it's invisible – like a *black nothingness* that arrived from outer space and tries to occupy your space of comfort. One could imagine that if you could rather hire an industrial vacuum cleaner to eradicate this *emptiness* it would probably just cause the machine to burn out or clog up and thereafter explode from the toxins and send harmful gases rushing directly into our eco-system. It would most definitely hit the headline news and cause our economy to collapse completely! But no it's not that descriptive.

It is difficult to even begin to explain the *sense* that it brings to our psyche, but yes it's there alright and we can't get away from it – I sure tried.

The more I became aware of *it* the harder I worked on my rose garden 'til eventually I could pin point each new leaf that had made its appearance within any given time.

The weeds started to irritate me – looking back they were actually *symbols* of my own life and put there as metaphors while they tried to communicate with me to get rid of the unnecessary agendas that were draining my soul's nutrients.

It came more suddenly than expected. One night David sat holding my hand and looked into my eyes and said "I can sense that you are unhappy, and I truly feel that you need to go and find what it is you are searching for. I am not asking you but telling you that you have to go back and be with Gareth".

Now Gareth has not been mentioned in this story before and yet he definitely played an extremely important role –in this case the roles have been featured behind the scenes - until now.

So here we go… Enter Gareth!

And the velvet curtains lift slowly and the crowds hold their breath as they anxiously wait for his appearance.

Countdown, three, two, one and '*Abracadabra*' there he stands, the man with the sparkling blue eyes that are full of love.

Humbly he stands under the spotlight as he bows to the audience
Wow it's a standing ovation, this play is heading straight for the Oscars!

Lo and behold this is the man that has stood by my side through thick and thin and loved me unconditionally to the point where he almost drove me crazy by being so over kind.
I tried, being the analytical person I am, to figure out what his ulterior motives were.
To me every man on this whole entire planet had a hidden agenda, therefore why not him? For those wishing to learn more about the '*behind the scenes*' acts, I suggest you read through my journal – titled '*Cinderbella's Unedited Journal*', soon to be published.
It's all there, note for note, word for word but you might have to add a little humour to it as it gets a bit gory and definitely should be censored. You might want to hide it away from any one that is under the age of 101, or squeamish about blood. Maybe even psychological classified '*cutters*' should be prohibited from these scenes as they will definitely pick up a few tips on how to cut your flesh and not die! Or decide that maybe 'you bunch of masochists, please donate those instruments to the scrap metal dump sites!' Oh and not to mention the numb housewife with the perfect flawless marriage – a definite no, no to for your viewing too! It's best that in your case you stay under your bushel and not come out into this scary world where there are real monsters!

So off to Gareth I went, much to my ego's horror!
I was supposed to be patching up my divorce, enjoying my emptiness and discarding the rose petals and not the weeds, so why

or why must this part of the play be appearing? It just didn't make sense!

Even though after my divorce Gareth and I had got to a stage that we grew to love each other, I had never lived with him on a permanent basis ever before and due to us being such good friends in the past, it was really awkward thinking that we could ever get into a serious relationship.

I remember how two months to date I drove out of the little village waving good-bye to David but yet fearfully my inner voice kept telling me that there would be no return.

This scared me.

I was not sure that this is what I wanted – how would I know for sure? Was this the *emptiness* that I was yearning for? How could the *emptiness* be replaced by another man?

I was too 'deep', too 'serious', too this and too that!

I felt insecure, awkward, afraid, all alone, and utterly stupid.

What would I say to Gareth?

I rehearsed my part continually. I had to *get it right*, no time for this very important actress, princess of all princesses, drama queen or any other labelled definition of mine to get damaged!

And so I practised the "Hi. Sorry to bug you." No, no that doesn't work! "Hi, it's me. How are you? Yes, I am on my way to you *again.* |" No, no that also doesn't do it! Oh goodness, how many times had I already stuffed this poor guy's life by going up and down and back and forth to my ex-husband!

Surely it would come to a point that enough is enough and he just wouldn't take any more of my drama.

Oh goodness, *mother Mary, baby Jesus, Pontius Pilot, whoever is out there* -   I could just feel that this was going to be extremely embarrassing.

It felt like I was going through menopause and needed to be admitted to a lifetime Spa where they could just pamper my broken wings and everything that was happening to me in this *real* life would then just disappear.

So what did I do? – I prayed. I prayed to whoever, whatever and anything that would actually help me! *"Hey, is there anybody out there, just nod if you can hear me, is there any one at home?"* I sure related to 'Pink Floyd' - now, more than ever before!

They were cloning me, instructing me, making me conform to what they thought I *needed to do*, how they dare tell me without asking me! All they wanted to do was put me into that giant sized mincing machine and shred me into tiny meaty pieces to satisfy their fat bellies! I could visually sense the way that they were 'doing this to me' in the same way that I had witnessed when viewing the movie called 'The Wall' – Pink Floyd.

The idiots! I became angry with David. He had to have an ulterior motive too! Why would he want me to go and be with Gareth and find that part of me that he had decided was an *'emptiness'*?

Men just never do that type of 'thing' like hand you over to another man. No they are warriors, protectors, providers – remember all the parts that he had allotted for himself – so why this sudden change?

Being better at writing than speaking I decided to mail him on my cellular phone and make it very clear that I was coming to him without any expectations. I wrote "Remember me, I am that self-supportive, independent woman that needs nothing or no one, and don't you forget it!"

But deep down inside behind all the external glitzy glamour, I needed a *sign*, one that would formulate this whole mess of mine into becoming a structural, orderly, factual conclusion. I desperately needed that God/goddess to turn up their hearing aids and show their faces! Maybe they didn't really exist either? Oh no, what if all the religious bedtime prayers were just another one of those Santa Claus fakes! Was I perhaps praying to no one or nothing for all these years of my life?

Cut, cut, cut this is getting too dramatic and way off the point. Let's get on with the show!

So down the gravel road I drive in my little white car that is filled to its brim with… yes, clothes. What else does a woman need in life when she is on her way to God knows where, to find her *emptiness*? The jewellery, rings and bangles were all part of the scene and not one had been forgotten behind.

And there he stood, my dear precious friend and man that I had grown to love unconditionally- Gareth. Arms stretched out with a warm smile on his face he gazed into my weary eyes – and then it happened.

As I looked at him I saw something totally unexpectedly – I saw *myself*. This sounds strange I am sure but this is *the truth and nothing but the truth so help me God/goddess.*

I have been here since then and who knows what the next tale will tell. I am not sure that I would be absurd enough to end it with the lines "*And they lived happily ever after*" but for now I know that every day brings a new challenge and I accept myself as a child of the universe that is brought to this planet to *learn*, *grow* and *share* my light with all those other souls that have gone through or are going through hardship in their relationship.

Hey we can do it; it gets better eventually. It's just about having the guts to say '*I Am!*' '*I am* a part of the light that is love and therefore I can do all things in God that strengthens me.' Accept that your soul will live on forever and therefore choose life not death while

140

journeying through this life in a vessel. Become that hero/heroine, it's your choice – I dare you!

PARANORMAL PERFECTION

Have you ever touched that space inside that frightens your logical human emotional conditioning?

It's the one that comes as a surprise when you begin to go behind your daily eyes

It's the space that beckons you through its silent voice to reach out and go yonder and recover its forgotten call.

It's the one that the mind denounces

and classifies it as 'insanity'

It's the heap that we sweep into a corner and label it as 'discard'

It's the space that we try and clothe our unconsciousness

and analyse it's causes

It's that space that we would rather hide from than face it in innocence and obey the calling

ACT TWENTY-NINE

--- *Two Halves Make One Whole* ---

Life is so full of unexpected events. We never know what tomorrow may hold but we do have the right to choose our present. We have one guarantee, and that is that we are all dying - but we also have the power within us to "walk our talk" - and live!

I have undergone an awe-inspiring metamorphosis, one that I never expected to happen in a trillion lifetimes, but what a ride it has been.

Every day I give thanks for the *gift* that has been given to me. If it was not for my own pain - how would I be able to feel others'?
The pain of a divorce is like a death, a loss that no words can begin to describe. I have lain on concrete floors crying out internally, to die – the blood from my self-induced cutting had become my pool of safety. I had taken on the pain so that no one else could cause me any more emotional harm.

Victoriously, this was not my delegated destiny, for what worth would my purpose on this earth have been? Yes I am blessed, whole; hold new hope and dreams in my heart, mind and soul to carry on once again, and become a witness to many, as I tell my new tale.

THE DAY MOON LAY UPSIDE DOWN

Staring up for reasons,
while aching down inside
wondering who had caused these changes of my life's
seasons,
Why had all hopes so blatantly died?

Life's commitments now broken,
we remove our marriage tokens
Tears swim down cracked face,
as we acknowledge that what remains
will only be bestowed upon us by His grace.

And as I stand alone I realise that no *next fix* – be they lover, friend or foe – can stand by me side while I undergo my own life's lessons - I have to stand *alone* and hold onto what life's *gifts* present to me, until such time that I arrive at the true destined home's doors and experience the truth of the *'welcome home forever'*.

The satin *veils* close and the viewer stands alone to analyse, criticise, applaud or silently absorb– but in the end – *does it really matter*?

The End

≈

---------- *Intermission* ----------

≈

Performance 2.

------ Mirroring the Self ------

INTRODUCTION TO THE MIRRORING THE *SELF* EXERCISES

As explained in the Prologue, this book is divided into two *'performances'*. The first *performance* was my own personal interpretation of the *game of life* and the now the second an additional/optional choice for you the reader to encounter your own *mirroring the Self exercises* as they begin to act out your *life's play*.

The 'mirroring the *Self* exercises' are designed to assist you with your own healing process. I have chosen to use art exercises which start from Exercise 5 for the readers to experiment with. These drawing/painting exercises can be integrated with your written journaling.

They should be done in sincerity and preferably not shown to any other parties, thereby allowing you a sense of 'owning' a form of *sacred space* . I have found that by journaling and doing my workbook during my time of my retreats truly assisted me to release the things that I could not easily speak about. They are not intended to become the beginning and end of your life's experiments but rather a means to allow yourself the time to become child-like again and remember how you once played.

In my own Book *of Self* - I too allowed myself to undergo an experience that I had only taught while having my Art School in Johannesburg - but had never been the student. It shifted me into a realm of understanding of what my *make-up* consisted of. Through it all, I realised that in order to be the teacher it was necessary to allow myself the 'gift' of becoming the student thereby '*to walk my talk rather than to just preach it!*'.

Therefore, I encourage you to challenge yourself to face your own *reflections* while you mirror yourself' through these exercises.

MIRRORING THE '*SELF*' EXERCISE 1

In your *Book of Self,* make a new heading for each of the following:

1.   Birth – 7 years' old
2.   7 – 14 years' old
3.   14 – 21 years' old
4.   Relationships

Under each of the above make sub-headings.   Write as much information down as possible about each timeframe. Take your time as these years are important and will be of useful information to all of your further "mirroring *self* exercises".

You may find that during a particular year in your life you cannot remember what events or emotions took place – that's not a problem - you don't have to get everything precise. You are dealing with timeframes and timeframes have emotions. If you are working on clues of what you did when you were for example five years old and all you can remember is that you wore a blue dress with a pink satin ribbon on your fifth birthday party for example – well then write that. If you hit a blockage at age six and cannot remember one single thing no matter how hard you try and go back to that timeframe – well that's perfect too. Just leave a space under that sub-heading – who knows somewhere in the near future you might have this astounding recall of *something* or *someone* that was a part of that particular time and then be able to go back and fill in all the details.   There are NO RIGHTS AND NO WRONGS in these exercises.

It is your own personal *Book of Self,* and therefore you can write what you want. You might choose to write down *emotional* words that express how you feel even though there is no *logical* reason why you think that you want to write them down – just do it – have no fear to express how you feel at any given timeframe. For example, you might be working on the timeframe of birth and cannot remember the faintest incident but in your heart you feel you want to write down the words "can't breathe" or "alive" or whatever – then write it! Many students in the past have experienced emotional changes and mood shifts whilst working with the issues of *self*, and mostly when any individual makes the decision to commit to their own *self*-healing process, they will come through as a *whole* person at the end. The trick to this lesson is to be real, let go and get it onto paper! Don't try and analyse it – well at least not at this early stage. We will be working with *self* from the very beginning to the very end, so be patient and *let go*!

When things get a bit too much to handle – breathe! Take a big breath in through your nose- fill your lungs and then breathe a long deep breath out of your mouth. Visualise a sense of peace and serenity flooding your whole entire body. Remind yourself that this is all about *you* and your *self*-healing. Be kind to yourself, love *you* and then let the emotional thoughts that may have aroused distress or discomfort flow out of your mind and body.

Work through the feelings - recall the smells, sights, sounds, tastes and sensations that you went through at any particular event. Write them down.

The best medicine in life is laughter – so if all else fails and you are almost at the verge of throwing up at some stage of your timeframe, just laugh. Laugh at the situation - laugh at the person involved -

laugh at yourself – just roll on the ground like a child – and laugh! It feels so much better when you get all these hidden agendas out.

Write and write and write – enjoy the first '*stage*' of your healing process.

MIRRORING THE '*SELF*' EXERCISE 2

In your *Book of Self,* write as much information down about the following aspects of YOURSELF.

Head them as:
1.   My passions
2.   My dislikes
3.   My greatest memories
4.   My worst memories
5.   My regrets

Relive these emotions. The more time and effort you put into these exercises, the more you will begin to get in touch with your *Self*.

Visualisation is about making use of all your senses: Feel and experience in a different way what you're seeing, hearing, feeling, tasting, and smelling.

Using art to express:

You will be inspired to create images and artworks that represent "YOU and YOUR IDENTITY". The following will give you a good **example** of how you can go about making the right choices:

You can decide to present your project in any of the different ways listed below depending on medium of your choice;
- As a newspaper
- As a magazine
- As a poster
- As a banner
- As a package
- Alternative medium of your choice.

Whatever one you select make sure that it contains a good selection of features that focus on your personal self – who you are, where you come from, your likes, your dislikes, your dreams, your aspirations and potential. The features you include should express positive feelings about yourself. This could include things that you would like to have or become. Here are some **ideas** to think about. Write down your suggestions in your sourcebook.
- my favourite things
- my religion
- my culture
- this is who I am
- this is who I would like to be
- this is what I love
- these are my achievements
- this is what I believe
- my aspirations
- my life
- my hero's
- my pride and joy
- happy moments

These ideas can be expressed through designing in the following ways:
- advertisement that expresses your uniqueness

-     a collage
-     features that show clearly how your dreams will come true
-     your family tree

What you put into your *Book of Self* book is up to you to decide on. Make it **expressive** and project a positive impression of who you really are!

MIRRORING THE '*SELF*' EXERCISE 3

This exercise will be a continuation of your exercise 2.

On a new page rewrite the same headings as exercise 2.

1.   My passions
2.   My dislikes
3.   My greatest memories
4.   My worst memories
5.   My regrets

Allow enough space for yourself to express your inner feelings.

Remember there is no right or wrong! We are each individual unique souls! We have the birth right to be true to ourselves, of which many of us have lost in the process of the various 'acts' of our life! We need to use these exercises to 'reclaim our birth rights' and become the whole human being once again!

In your *Book of Self,* write as much information down about the following aspects:

1.   My passions: What aspects do you feel that you have lost out on due to the many various circumstances that did not permit you to have the opportunity to accomplish doing them.

2.   My dislikes: what type of reactions do your dislikes bring out in you? Write them down. How does reaction make you feel? Example: *I dislike untidy spaces; it tends to make me feel like I want*

to 'fix' them and 'create a sense of order'. Now analyse why you think that these reactions are stirred in you? Example: *I think that my reactions are stirred in me be because I feel 'out of control of things'.* Work through all your 'dislikes' and deeply analyse them.

3.   My greatest memories: question yourself whether or not you are willing to make new 'great memories' in your present situation. List them. Express them through collecting photographs out of magazines etc., drawing them, writing about them etc. Really get in touch with them as though they are actually happening!

4.   My worst memories: Go back to the pages that you wrote on this topic. Analyse them for a while so that your memory is refreshed. Now spend a few minutes in your quiet space and 'see' yourself safe, protected and surrounded by a beautiful ray of white light - your very own care-taker! Ensure that you are completely comfortable. This exercise should be done in a manner that you 'pretend that you are the viewer of a movie'. Whatever scenes you see should be considered as not real. You are not the actor only part of the audience. It might take a little practice and if you feel that you are not ready for it quiet yet, remember that you can always return at a later stage. It is however recommended that as many of the exercises are practiced as this will enable you to promote your own growth.

Begin by focusing on your breathing. There are many books and internet resources that are available to assist you with these techniques if you are not already familiar with them.

Now in your 'mind's eye' visualise each one of your worst memories that you originally wrote down. Remember you are only the viewer! Now while watching your movie 'feel' how that actor was feeling during that specific scene. Detach yourself from becoming too emotional as you are not intended to be the actor! In the case that emotions do arise, breathe them out with deep long breaths and remind yourself that they are not real. Don't attach any value to them, just see them for what they are – a play, a movie, a particular scene. Listen carefully to what the actor/s are saying in the play. Do you have any emotions that stir up because you can relate? Write down your emotions after each scene and then move on to the next movie.

Visualise a big white X that pushes the "delete' button and wipes clean all existence of these particular movies. Just know that it has served you no purpose and they are not necessary to watch again. Work through each one of your worst memories in the above describe way until you have completed as many as possible. Once completed take long, slow healing breathes and feel the tranquillity that surrounds you after you have 'got rid of things' that weighed you down. Through time there have been many religious rituals that have helped to align men and woman with the beauty of life. In these contemporary times society seems to have lost those magical customs and we have to make the effort in our everyday life to ensure that we are 'in balance'. There are so many emotionally unstable woman and men out in this life today that are searching for that inner peace and balance. Where do they turn to - drugs, television, affairs, pornography? By taking the few little steps to the 'desire' to heal your 'wounded self' can only become a positive step in this crazy world we call Earth.

5.   My regrets: this exercise should be done in the same way as the above. Visualisation has been scientifically proven to be of great assistance to the human well-being.

MIRRORING THE 'SELF' EXERCISE 4

In this lesson it is recommended that you select a place of interest. Suggestions:

-        If you enjoy shopping malls, then this would be a place where your interests can be explored.

-        You might be a person who prefers nature – then any place that you relate to should become your place of exploration.

Be creative, and dress the part. Become the part of this new 'play'. Imagination is one avenue that many of us have lost. I am sure that when you were younger it was a natural instinct. See yourself as having the freedom to be whoever you want to be once again. Dress for the occasion! If society expectations and monotony really don't appeal to you, why not dress in an outfit that will express your feelings? You could try going to a shopping mall in your oldest clothes or if you really want to get to know more about the 'creatures of habit' that live on this planet – try dressing up extremely smart and go for a walk on the beach. Make it a fun exercise.

1.   Start by writing down a few of your interests and/or places that you feel that you would enjoy going to.

2.   Select a date and time that is suitable.

3.   Decide on what 'statement' you want to make for yourself. We are all unique and many will feel that just going into nature or a shopping mall dressed in the correct manner – is more suitable for their personality trait. There is no right or wrong, and how you 'feel' at the given time is totally dependable on where, how or what you wish to 'say' or 'be'. Remember that most of these lessons are 'plays and acts'. The scenes should be carried out as though they are not 'real'. The lessons are not intended to make your life a misery - life is already stressful enough- they are here to encourage you to 'play' and 'see life for what is 'is', 'was' and 'could be'. The amount of fun that you can have is all dependable on your attitude. Loosen up if you need to. Laugh at the 'mess' and 'chuck out the rest'!

4.   You can select a few of the following items to take along
with you
-       Recording device
-       Camera
-       Writing pad
-       Drawing pad and pencils

MIRRORING THE '*SELF*' EXERCISE 5

Using art to express:

WHERE DO I START?
SUGGESTED BASIC FORMAT
A substantial, good quality 3A sketchbook size or a file that can be
extended and new pages added as the process progresses.
A smaller format cheap notepad
Small telephone message pad sized scraps of paper, this you can
carry around with you at all times and jot down ideas or thoughts
that come to mind.

Work through as many of the following activities as possible. They
are here for your own benefit and if done will help you with your
own personal creative processes in the future. Do not be scared to
experiment! Write down your thoughts, they are YOUR thoughts
and there is no right or wrong.

IS THIS AN INTERESTING SURFACE TO WORK ON?
Find 10 different surfaces which could function as a separate new
page i.e. a surface for drawing on.

Materials might include: Canvas, poplin, plastic, old letters, a sheet made of sellotape, dried paper mache (mash), x-ray plate, newsprint, photographs, and so on. A surface could also be constructed of a number of pieces of material. A monoprint page, handmade paper, compressed organic fibre or tree bark may present alternative options as drawing surfaces.

Find a fragment of a different potential drawing surface, a third the size of the original format and paste, paste or fix it to the original surface. Select the fragment carefully to contrast with the surface that it is attached to. Consider tone, texture or material contrast. Document the processes.

MIRRORING THE '*SELF*' EXERCISE 6

MATERIAL / EQUIPEMENT NEEDED: different surfaces, visual references

Using art to express:

Scribbling the everyday

This should ideally become a habitual activity, continued as necessary, probably indefinitely. One often collects bits and pieces from one's everyday environment. These could be notes about things you have seen, lists, labels from consumer objects, newspaper clippings, surfaces and textures which attract you, old personal photos or bits of letters, stamps, doilies or paper serviettes, sweet papers, doodles or rough drawings on scraps of paper, business cards, greeting cards, advertisements, etc. Identify for yourself your personal areas of interest: colour, surface, texture, personal memorabilia, shapes, patterning, the physical substance, the craziness, or whatever. Include these bits of bric-a-brac onto your drawing surfaces according to some scheme. The scheme may range from colour considerations, forms of contrast, consistent placing on the page each time (composition), to complete randomness. In so doing, try to beware of your criteria of choice each time, so that you start to accumulate a personal logic of how you make sense of things, how you make organisational decisions.

Start a collection of found surfaces. Start a collection of personally constructed surfaces (doodles, lists, names of people, places and things, for example) on the smallest format notepad you have. Get used to putting down even the most apparently insignificant idea you have as directly as possible in some tangible form: it may take no more than 10 seconds! Some of the items could be shredded, crumpled or reconstituted in some other way BEFORE the fragments or remains are inserted or attached onto each surface.

MIRRORING THE '*SELF*' EXERCISE 7

MATERIAL / EQUIPEMENT NEEDED: koki, fine liner, pencil or pen and ink, or any of the above media you have discovered

Using art to express:

The aim of this exercise is to recognise the personal and historical characteristics and STYLES of different drawing conventions. There are many different ways of drawing the same thing! Using either a heavy Koki, fine liner, pencil or pen and ink, or any of the above media you have discovered in above activities, make a good imitation/copy or drawings or any images which you like, one on each drawing surface. The image may be from a mechanical manual, magazine, art book, comic strip or illustration. Look at the different scales of the copies which you make (for example, one drawing might be only within the confines of a small collaged fragment inside your page, and others may extend over the various different surfaces of a whole page). Pay very careful attention to making as accurate a copy as you can, given the limitations of your surfaces and the materials used in making the drawing. Sometimes using very clumsy or difficult implements can help the spontaneity and looseness of the drawing made.

REMEMBER: DRAWING LOOSELY IS NOT THE SAME AS GENERALISED OR SLOPPY RENDERING

IMAGES, COLLAGE ELEMENTS, TRANSFERS, ETC. MAY BE SUPERIMPOSED AND OVERLAP. THE DIFFERENT ELEMENTS MUST BE INTEGRATED IN THE FINAL STAGE

MIRRORING THE 'SELF' EXERCISE 8

MATERIAL / EQUIPEMENT NEEDED: magazines, cotton-wool, thinners, paper, pencil or spoon.

Using art to express:

Thinners transfer

Choose a part of the surface that seems empty or has a blank hole" for this exercise. Take a texture image or colour from a magazine and place it in position on the surface. Using cotton-wool, wet the image **thoroughly** with some *Thinners*, and apply pressure directly by rubbing with the cotton-wool on the BACK of the image, or **indirectly** by rubbing with a pencil or the back of a spoon until the image is transferred onto your page. This may also be process for rendering line or **texture,** so that only those parts in contact with the pencil actual get transferred.

MIRRORING THE *'SELF'* EXERCISE 9

MATERIAL / EQUIPEMENT NEEDED: paper, pencil crayons.

Using art to express:

Words as colour shapes

Choose a' clean' or 'thin' area in a drawing. Decide on a set of colours or tones that will represent the mood of the word. While repeating the word several times slowly, draw a shape or shapes that will capture the expressive quality of the sound and the word. Rework the shape while repeating the word - add marks, textures and lines.

LISTEN TO THE SHAPE OF THE WORD

MIRRORING THE *SELF* EXERCISE 10

MATERIAL / EQUIPEMENT NEEDED: paper, different coloured Koki pens, CD player

Using art to express:

In time, on time, all the time

Select ten words -
Format: 10 to 12 small scraps of paper
Medium: Different coloured Koki pens

Decide on who will bring the following to class:
CD player
Moody music.

Activity instructions:
Select various pieces of moody music. While listening to the music, interpret it by creating a variety of marks on one of the pieces of paper. Listen intensely and try to capture the rhythm, the harmony, beat and flow of the composition. 'Dance' on the paper with marks, lines scratches, dabs, shapes and movements. Try to obtain a good translation of the composition in visual terms. Select different colours, Koki's or pastels for different compositions. Soft hazy colours and scumbled shapes can be juxtaposed with sharp, scratchy lines. The pieces of paper can be pasted to the surface of a drawing
Or parts of the drawings can be repeated or copied onto the drawings.

YOUR VISUAL MUSIC SCORE CAN ACT AS A CATALYST WHICH BINDS THE DIFFERENT COMPONENTS OF ON THE SURFACE TOGETHER.

MIRRORING THE 'SELF' EXERCISE 11

Using art to express:

MIND MAPPING

Research is the best way to go about this exercise. Here is an example of how one can find out more about yourself through **brainstorming – mind mapping.**

Write down a word that identifies with your subject matter that you have chosen and then do a mind map.

From this word, other words are added on. Doing a mind-map helps you identify what the narrative (story) of your artwork is.

Now do a mind-map, using the word "Self". See what words you come up with and identify what narrative you wish to work with. After using the word 'self' try another word using 'Identity'. Other words that will be important to brainstorm are: 'Heritage' and 'Conservation'.

In a mind map, one word is used as a central idea. The first 10 words that come to mind are written down on each arm/extension and then the next 20 words, et cetera.

This is a process of WORD ASSOCIATIONS.

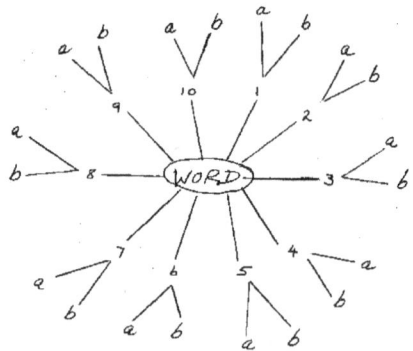

MIRRORING THE 'SELF' EXERCISE 12

Using art to express:

IDENTITY

The following will give you a good **example** of how you can go about making the right choices:

You can decide to tackle your project in any of the different ways listed below depending on medium of your choice;

- As a newspaper
- As a magazine
- As a poster
- As a banner
- As a package
- Alternative medium of your choice.

Whatever one you select make sure that it contains a good selection of features that focus on your personal **self** – who you are, where you come from, your likes, your dislikes, your dreams, your aspirations and potential. The features you include should express positive feelings about yourself. This could include things that you would like to have or become.

Here are some **ideas** to think about. Write down your suggestions in your sourcebook.

- my favourite things
- my religion
- my culture

- this is who I am
- this is who I would like to be
- this is what I love
- these are my achievements
- this is what I believe
- my aspirations
- my life
- my hero's
- my pride and joy
- happy moments

These ideas can be expressed through designing in the following ways:
- advertisement that expresses your uniqueness
- a collage
- features that show clearly how your dreams will come true
- your family tree

What you put into your sourcebook is up to you to decide on. Make it **expressive** and project a positive impression of who you really are!

Whichever way you decide to go about, make sure that the following are included:
- Previews of forthcoming attractions, be they art, music, movement or drama.
- An interview with a guest artist, musician or actor
- Reviews on plays or concerts

When doing your project be selective in your images.

Think about the format that you wish to present your artwork in.

Think about your layout. Do research on layout for artworks

Your work should have a sense of balance to it.

Experiment with different mediums

Find out about the elements of art and write a description on each element (line, shape, tone, texture, colour and form)

Research work on composition

Find out interesting facts about artists that work in similar mediums as you have chosen. Take Photostats of their artworks and paste them into your sourcebook.

This project focuses on you and your responses to yourself in the form of **VISUAL SELF-ANALYSIS**. This will include your physical make-up and psychological state-of-being, your public image and your "private person".

There are many possibilities in this project. You will therefore need to define your own parameters and areas of interest. Using preparatory research methodologies develop exploratory processes which will assist you in defining your specific interests or a focus within the broader area of investigation.

IDENTITY - who a person is or what a thing is.

Artists have always been fascinated with portraiture and the self-portrait. Besides the single figure, the human condition and human behavior will continue to be a central issue in art and there **will** always be artists who concentrate on the idiosyncrasies of individuals, pathos and suffering, brutality and the horrors of war, psychological states of mind, pleasures and festivities, to name a few.

Through the self-portrait the artist is able to comment and meditate on him/her self within a particular place and time and in response to particular conditions. The self-portrait goes beyond "likeness" or mere representation. It is able to express and reflect on the "whole" person by an interpretation of a person's personality. Irony, satire and humour are often employed in these interpretations as well as physical imperfections, as ways of portraying the artist's sense of self.

Possible choices of subject matter are:

Your face

Your full figure

Do 3 expressive self-portrait drawings - head and shoulders or full figure. Consider the spatial context - that is, the way in which you treat the negative space. You could also use the multiple image.

Medium:

1) quick ink and jik stain remover

2) shoe polishes, stains, oxides

3) acrylic paint (black, white and gray)

Format: smooth cartridge or brown paper

Size: + A2 for each drawing

MIRRORING THE '*SELF*' EXERCISE 13

Using art to express:

Compare and contrast
In your *Book of Self*, write down any ideas that you may wish to explore:

CONSIDER: 3-dimensional form and structure; body language; gestures; twisting; stretching; crouching; limpness; tensions; space; context; body prints; body painting; wrapping; scarring; tattoos; stitching

1. TAKE INTO CONSIDERATION "A CONTEXT" FOR YOUR SELF-PORTRAITS
2. Comparing all your drawings, which works convey something particular about yourself?
3. What medium has potential for your ideas?
4. How does body language help your work?
5. Can technique alone convey ideas?
6. Would the scale of the work alter the meaning?
7. Can light alter the meaning?
8. Have you considered a shaped format?
9. Have you considered portraying only parts of the body?
10. Have you considered fragments?
11. Do you see yourself as vulnerable, safe, domineering, meek, funny, moody, calm, excitable, volatile, depressed, frantic, angry, frustrated, happy exuberant, serene, shy, bold, etcetera.
12. Do the photographs or drawings capture any of these expressions?

MIRRORING THE '*SELF*' EXERCISE 14

MATERIAL / EQUIPEMENT NEEDED: sketchbooks, journals, planners and a portfolio, pencils etc.

Using art to express:

Exercise 1:
INSTRUCTIONS

1. Make a series of 3 self-portraits in which you express:
- exuberance or excitability
- depression or aggression
- vulnerability or dominance
 - fragility or strength
 - age
- or alternative concepts

AVOID ILLUSTRATIVENESS AND SENTIMENTALITY

Exercise 2:
INSTRUCTIONS

Make a drawing using your own image as the subject matter in which you explore one of the following:
- the surreal
- the absurd
- psychosis
- or an alternative of your choice
- fragmentation
- bondage
- satire

Consider all your experimentations.

Medium: own choice
Format: own choice
Size: own choice

And so your journey continues – no right, no wrong just keep going forward and travel on your life's journey until the day we all meet and become the 'I AM'.

-        Painting, Mixed Medium, painted while searching for
Self. Deanne Kim 2001

171

Titled Aborted life. Drawing. Mixed Medium

-Deanne Kim 2001

-       Sequence of the Titled *Unscarred.* Mixed Medium,
painted while searching of *Self. Deanne Kim 2001*

-        Sequence of the Titled *Unscarred, Mixed* Medium,
(Painted while searching of *Self*).   *Deanne Kim 2001*

-        Sequence of: 'Unveiled',
Mixed Medium.   - (Painted while searching for *Self*.)
Deanne Kim 2008

175

-       Sequence of: 'Unveiled',
Mixed Medium.   (Painted while searching for *Self*.)
Deanne Kim 2008

-------------*Epilogue*--------------

And as I close this chapter of my own life's experiences, I am humbled and grateful to know that every step of the way to date, I have been guided by the Light that promised to *come and fetch me one day* as a little girl.

Whilst writing this book based on my past I was given the opportunity to explore and express my *Self* and make peace with many Acts.

I must admit that it was difficult doing the final editing -as I did not feel I wanted to change the way it was written more than eight or so years ago so instead chose to leave it for what it was.

In closure to this Performance I now wish to set my life's lessons free to become '*gifts*' to those that may need to read what I have learnt and look forward to writing my new book titled *The Greatest Love Story*

Blessed Be -
Deanne Kim

And so my journey continues- - - - x - - - x - - x - - x

www.ingramcontent.com/pod-product-compliance
Lightning Source LLC
Chambersburg PA
CBHW061719020426
42331CB00006B/999